Countryknits
for Kids

Countryknits for Kids

Complete patterns and instructions
for 24 casual sweaters
inspired by American folk designs

Stephen & Carol Huber

Artwork by Chesca Sheldon
Photographs of sweaters by Schecter Lee

E. P. Dutton   New York

Book design by Marilyn Rey

10 9 8 7 6 5 4 3 2

CONTENTS

INTRODUCTION

We are thrilled by, and grateful for, your wonderful response to our first knitting book, *Countryknits*. We thought we had some good ideas for sweaters, and we are so delighted that you have loved them, shared your thoughts and good wishes with us, and better yet—have knit them. We are truly touched and encouraged by the generous support given in your calls and letters. What fun!

For those of you who may not be familiar with us and our first knitting book, we'd like to tell you a little about ourselves. We are antiques dealers, specializing in textiles of the 17th through the 19th centuries—both English and American. We have handled some wonderful fabrics, needleworks, woven blankets and bedcovers, samplers, etc., which have inspired many of our designs. We live in a 1685 gambrel house in the country, and have turned one of our barns into a design and work studio where we create the patterns for knitting, and make kits for our mail-order sweater business. Because of the antiques business, we quite often find ourselves in England, and from this association came the development of our knitting core in England, where the sweaters are knit for those people who do not have the time—or heaven forbid don't know how to knit—to make their own.

We started our knitting venture a couple of years ago with a few patterns that were very well received: people saw them, wanted them, and off we went. The business, which we started as a hobby, has grown into a full-time venture for both of us, several part-time employees, and with kits and books being sent all over the world. This small-time "mom and pop" operation gets bigger by the day, and we are thrilled that you knitters have given us such a big reception.

So many of you immediately after looking at our first volume requested patterns for children that we have brought together a selection we think appropriate to the country flair, casual and classic look we've captured in our first endeavor. Many of these patterns will look familiar to those of you who have knit our sweaters before. The Country Goose, the number one all-time favorite, is scaled down for sizes 8 to 14, and a little version has been designed as a jacket for the toddler set. The Basket Quilt, Patchwork, Schoolhouse, and some of the geometric designs we thought appropriate for children, are all here. But along with these old classics, we've introduced lots of new patterns: Buckingham Palace Guards, Rag Rugs, a Rockinghorse, a Christmas Goose, Moored Boats for your sailors, to name a few. Venturing somewhat into the twentieth century, but maintaining our country style, we've included an Art Deco Flamingo and Palm, and Flying Kites. After all, country kids go to the city too, and they need to have something snappy to wear. All in all we think this is a fun, interesting, and challenging collection of designs that you will enjoy knitting, and the youngsters will love wearing.

We would like to take a little space here to give some very special thanks to the people who are helping make both the designs and the books so successful. First, a big and very proud thank you to our daughter Chesca, who is a large part of this operation: she designs (the Rabbit is all hers, as is the Flamingo), graphs patterns, opens mail, labels catalogues, fills orders, answers the phone, comes home from college to help type names when we get too swamped, and encourages us when we sometimes wonder if we're going about this the right way. She's a super partner.

Second, a very special thank you to our editor Cyril Nelson, who has been so wonderfully encouraging and even inspirational at times. We are so fortunate to have someone who understands this project and is so genuinely happy for us.

Finally, thank you, knitters, so much for your excitement over our patterns and your terrific response. There would be no purpose in any of this if it wasn't for you. We are so pleased that we're doing something you like. Just to share a few of the comments with all of you. Our readers have written:

> "...thank you for sending the book. It is so lovely. I have had a knit shop for 31 years and I can say it's the prettiest book I have ever seen."

> "...the book is sensational!!! 10 came in on Monday and they were all gone by Wednesday."

> "...congratulations on putting together such a stunning collection."

> "...This is a terrible thing you've done to me! I want to make all the sweaters!"

> "...I have never in all my 35 years of knitting seen such a beautiful, beautiful, beautiful book. My daughter of course escaped with it. Now I want another."

So there you have it, our fun and effort and your response. Here's to knitting more wonderful family heirlooms—and we do hope you will enjoy this second book as much as the first.

KNITTING NOTES

ABBREVIATIONS:

alt	alternate
beg	begin(ning)
cont	continue
dec	decrease
inc	increase
K	knit
P	purl
st	stitch
st st	stockinette stitch
tog	together

TENSION OR GAUGE:

These terms are often used interchangeably. They refer to how tightly or how loosely the knitter is knitting compared with the gauge given in the pattern or by the yarn manufacturer. The gauge is the number of stitches *and* the number of rows to equal one inch. It is very important in knitting to keep this gauge correct as a mistake is multiplied with each row and the pattern will become either elongated or compressed. The horizontal gauge is the number of stitches to make one inch and determines the finished chest size. The vertical gauge is the number of rows to equal one inch and determines the finished length.

Knit a tension square before you begin any garment. Work a 2-inch square in stockinette stitch. Lay it flat and carefully measure the rows and stitches to equal one inch in each direction. If your work is larger than the specified gauge your tension is too loose and you should move down to a smaller needle. If your measurement comes out smaller, your tension is too tight and you should move to a larger needle.

DETERMINING AND ALTERING SIZE:

To determine the size garment to knit, take a chest measurement and add 2 to 4 inches depending on how tight or how loose you want the sweater to fit. (Remember, wool tends to stretch a bit.) Compare your tension with the gauge and make any needle corrections. Take measurements for the following: length of finished garment from underarm, length of finished garment from middle of shoulder, and length of finished sleeve to underarm. Compare your measurements with those given for the pattern and lengthen or shorten as needed.

SIZING:

(1) Measure chest. (2) Add 2 to 4 inches (depending on how loose you want the sweater). (3) Divide total measurement by 2. (4) Multiply this number by the number of sts in one inch. This gives the number of sts needed for front and back. (5) Subtract 8 from above number for ribbing. (6) Cast on number of sts from step 5. Work in ribbing for K1, P1 for 3 inches and increase 8 sts in next row using st st. (7) Follow graph, deleting or adding pattern from graph at sides. Work to underarm. (8) Measure from underarm to desired length. (9) Subtract ribbing. (10) Multiply by number of rows per inch. This gives the number of rows for desired underarm length. (11) Adjust graph by adding or deleting as necessary. (12) Measure desired length to neck edge of shoulder. (13) Subtract underarm length. (14) Multiply by the number of rows per inch. This gives the number of rows for desired length from underarm to shoulder. (Allow a little extra for sufficient arm movement.) (15) Unless you are knitting a very large (over 34 inches), or very

small (under 24 inches) garment, the neck will not need adjustment. However, sts can be added or deleted and neck edge moved in or out. (16) Shoulders will have the number of sts determined by the number cast on at beginning. At underarm bind off according to chart and follow decreasing. (17) At shoulder bind off as pattern shows. (18) Measure length of sleeve to underarm. (19) Subtract ribbing. (20) Multiply by the number of rows per inch. Adjust pattern by adding or deleting rows. (21) Follow pattern for top of shoulder. (22) For small sizes (24 inches and under) delete 2 to 3 sts each side of sleeve pattern. For large sizes (34 inches and over) add 2 to 3 sts each side of sleeve pattern.

An alternative method of adjusting the size is to increase the size of the garment by using bulkier yarns or to decrease the size of the sweater by using finer yarns. The yarn-gauge chart shows many different yarns, a needle number, and the number of stitches per inch and the number of rows per inch. Check your gauge with the graph to determine the size garment you will end up with by following the charted graph with a different yarn.

GRAPHS:

The patterns in this book are all charted on graphs. Each square represents one stitch. The patterns are shown in color, or in black and white. The black-and-white have different symbols to distinguish the colors. Adjustments can be made by adding or deleting rows, or moving the side seam and armhole line in or out. Increase and decrease stitches are indicated on the sides, and binding off is designated by decreasing more than one stitch.

ADAPTING PATTERNS TO DIFFERENT SWEATERS:

Many of the patterns in this book lend themselves to more than one sweater shape. The Country Goose crewneck pullover, for example, is also shown as a cardigan. Other designs can be changed by using the outline from one sweater and the design graph from another. Cardigan possibilities include: Irish Chain, Double Irish Chain, Flying Geese, Patchwork Sampler, and Windowpane. V-neck vests or pullovers suggested are: Irish Chain, Double Irish Chain, Flying Geese, Diamonds, and Windowpane. Possibilities are endless by using combinations of patterns and different yarns.

YARN-GAUGE CHARTS:

The yarn-gauge charts are included so that one can quickly convert a pattern from one type of yarn to another. Heavy-weight wools can be used for sweaters calling for sport-weight yarn, or vice versa, by adjusting the pattern according to the above directions and using the yarn-gauge charts as a guide to needle size and tension. It's fun; by all means experiment!

KNITTING THE GARMENT:

Here are a few general notes on the actual knitting of the sweater. For a neater edge, whenever possible slip the first stitch and knit into the back of the last stitch on every row. This will create a neater edge, and it will be easier to sew and match up the pattern.

Do not join yarn in the middle of a row; it usually shows and creates a bulky area. Join at the beginning of the row with a new ball and use both ends for sewing seams later.

An especially important note about the sweater patterns in this book. Do not carry the yarn across the back of the sweater when working pattern motifs. Use bobbins (or small balls) and change yarn with each color change simply by looping the first yarn around the new color and continuing with the new yarn. This is very important with heavy yarns as they tend to pucker and become bulky.

SEWING TOGETHER:

To join the garment together, use the same yarn it was knitted with. Use a running stitch and go through each stitch on each side of the seam. (A back stitch makes the seam bulky, and an overcast stitch is not as neat.) Make sure not to pull the yarn too tightly and secure the ends of the seam with a double stitch. Weave in all ends two or three inches before cutting. Do not knot sewing yarns.

BLOCKING:

Wool sweaters should be pressed when completed so that the seams will lie flat. When blocking, use a damp cloth and a warm iron. Lay the seams flat and press down with the iron but do not go back and forth. Wool tends to mat and become shiny if pressed too long. It is easier to sew the shoulder and sleeve/armhole seams first and then press before sewing the long sleeve and side seam.

WASHING:

Hand-knitted garments should be hand-washed. Use a mild detergent and lukewarm water. Do not rub, wring, twist, scrub, or let the water run directly on the garment. Gently push the sweater into the water and lightly agitate it up and down. Do not soak for long as this mats wool. Rinse thoroughly, squeeze slightly, and roll between two towels to remove excess water. Lay flat and smooth back into shape.

YARN-GAUGE CHART

Group A Yarns	Needle Size	Gauge
George Picaud Lambswool	5	7 sts 8½ rows
Columbia-Minerva Scotch Fingering	4	7 sts 9 rows
Columbia-Minerva Nantuck Fingering	4	7 sts 9 rows

Group B Yarns	Needle Size	Gauge
Columbia-Minerva Featherweight Knitting Worsted	5	6 sts 7½ rows
Columbia-Minerva Shetland Wool	5	6 sts 7½ rows
Bernat Berella Sportspun	5	6 sts 8 rows
Picaud Laine et Coton	5	6 sts 8 rows
Chat Botte Petrouchka	4	6 sts 8 rows
3 Suisses Suizy DK	5	6 sts 6½ rows
Patons Clansman DK	4	6½ sts 7½ rows
S. & C. Huber's American Classic 100% cotton	5	6 sts 6½ rows

Group C Yarns	Needle Size	Gauge
S. & C. Huber's American Classic 100% wool, Fisherman 2-ply	6	5 sts 6½ rows
Galler's Olympic-Supra 100% wool	8	5 sts 6 rows
Unger Natuurwol	6	5 sts 6 rows
Pingouin Comfortable Sport	6	5 sts 6½ rows
Galler's Cotton Express	6	5 sts 6 rows
Galler's Parisian Cotton RBC	6	5 sts 6 rows
Columbia-Minerva Nantuck Sports	6	5 sts 7 rows
Bernat Sesame 4	8	5 sts 7 rows
Bernat Berella "4"	8	5 sts 7 rows
Galler's Pony, 100% cotton	5	5½ sts 6½ rows
Unger's Britania	6	5½ sts 7 rows
Lister-Lee Motoravia DK	5	5½ sts 8 rows
Phildar Sagittaire	4	5½ sts 8 rows

Group D Yarns	Needle Size	Gauge
Sunbeam Aran	7	4½ sts 6 rows
Columbia-Minerva Knitting Worsted	8	4½ sts 6 rows
Columbia-Minerva Heatherglo	8	4½ sts 6 rows
Nantuck 4-ply Knitting Worsted	8	4½ sts 6 rows
Nantuck Dimension	8	4½ sts 6 rows
Nantuck Spectra	8	4½ sts 6 rows
Reverie	8	4½ sts 6 rows

SIZE CHART

(Number of stitches needed for the front or the back)

Finished Size	20	22	24	26	28	30	32	34
Group A Yarns	70	77	84	91	98	105	112	119
Group B Yarns	60	66	72	78	84	90	96	102
Group C Yarns	50	55	60	65	70	75	80	85
Group D Yarns	45	50	54	59	63	68	72	77

NEEDLE CONVERSION CHART

Metric U.K. & Australia	U.K., Australia Canada, S. Africa	U.S.A.
2	14	00
2¼	13	0
2¾	12	1
3	11	2
3¼	10	3
3¾	9	4
4	8	5
4½	7	6
5	6	7
5½	5	8
6	4	9
6½	3	10
7	2	10½
7½	1	11
8	0	12
9	00	13
10	000	15

Sampler Vest

SAMPLER VEST

A tiny version of our much-loved sampler crewneck. Simplified for a quick "Country" look, this little vest is fun for youngsters who are learning, or already know their ABC's.

MATERIALS: 3 to 4 oz. of main color in sport-weight yarn, Shetland, or yarn recommended for gauge below. Small amounts of red, dark brown, blue, dark green, light green, light brown, and pink.

NEEDLES: Size 3 and 5. One set of double-point needles, size 3.

GAUGE: 6 sts = 1 inch; 7–7½ rows = 1 inch.

SIZE: These directions are for a size 1. Changes for sizes 2 and 4 are given in parentheses. Finished chest measurement of sweater is 19½ (21½, 23½) inches.

NOTE: This sweater may be made with thicker yarn and larger needles. A heavier sport-weight, cotton, or 2-ply worsted yarn worked on size 4 and 6 needles with a gauge of 5 sts to the inch and 6 rows to the inch will give finished chest sizes of 23 (25½, 28) inches.

FRONT: With size 3 needles, cast on 54 (60, 66) sts. Work in K1, P1, ribbing for 1½ inches. Change to size 5 needles and working in st st increase 4 sts evenly spaced across first row. Continue in st st and work the charted design, binding off and decreasing as indicated. Place the 14 sts in center of front on holder to be picked up later for neck ribbing.

BACK: Work to match front, continuing the bottom border around the back. Use upper line of graph for back neck opening. Place the center 16 sts on a holder for neck ribbing.

Sew shoulder and side seams, leaving one shoulder partly opened if buttons are desired.

NECK: With size 3 double-point needles, and right side facing, pick up 48 sts including sts on front and back holders and work in K1, P1, ribbing for ¾ inch, leaving side and shoulder open for button closure. Bind off loosely in K1, P1 ribbing. Single-edge crochet around both sides of open section of neck and shoulder. Add single-crochet buttonholes and buttons.

ARMHOLES: With size 3 double-point needles, and right side facing, pick up 56 (62, 62) sts and work in K1, P1, ribbing for ¾ inch. Bind off loosely in ribbing.

Weave in loose threads from pattern work.

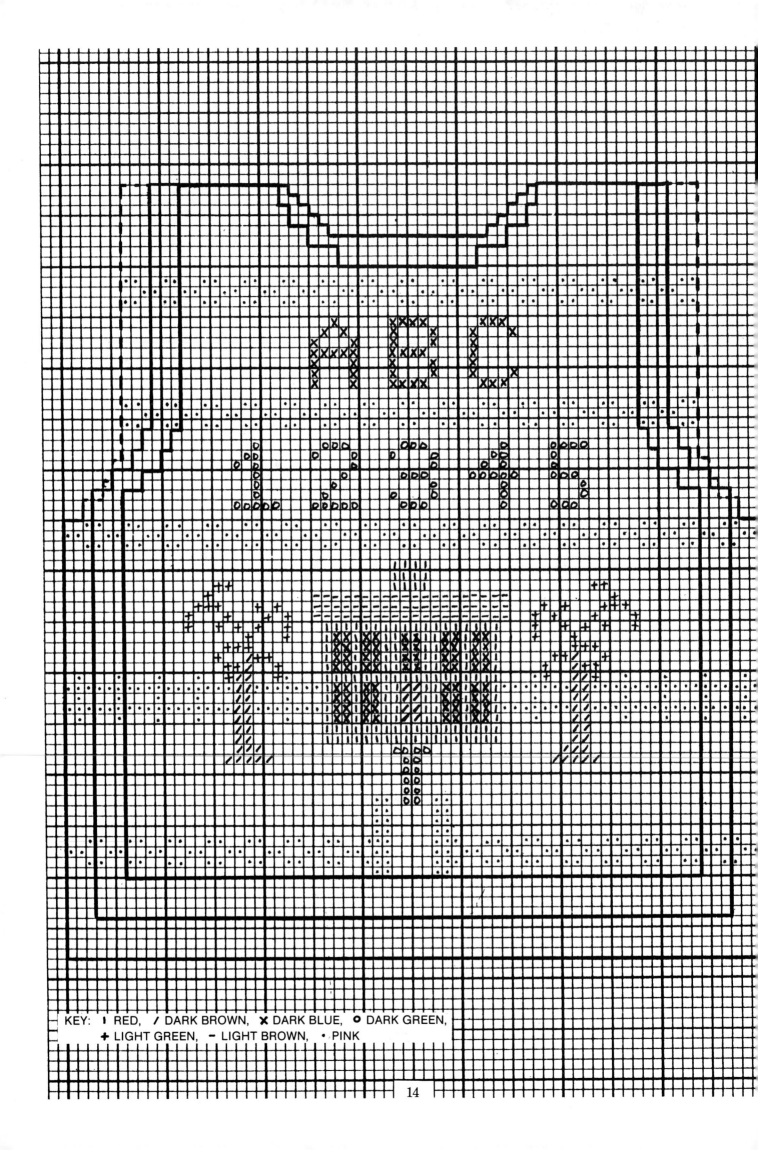

Country Goose Jacket

COUNTRY GOOSE JACKET

A great "Country-look" jacket for sizes up to 8. The response to our adult Country Goose sweater was terrific, so we did it in a smaller version for sizes 8 to 14 (see pages 60–61), and here it is specially rendered for the under-8 set. It's a wonderful sweater and a show-stopper wherever it goes!

MATERIALS: 12 oz. off-white or other background color in knitting-worsted-weight yarn, 2 oz. light blue, 2 oz. dark green. Small amounts of red, light green, gold, and brown.

NEEDLES: Size 7. One size E crochet hook.

GAUGE: 4½ sts = 1 inch; 6½–7 rows = 1 inch.

SIZE: These directions are for a size 2. Size 4 directions are given in parentheses. Finished chest measurement is 19½ (21½) inches.

FRONT and BACK: The body of the sweater is knit in one piece. With size 7 needles cast on 87 sts. Work in K1, P1, first row. Second row K. Repeat these two rows until piece measures 2¾ inches ending with wrong side. K next row, increasing 1 st at the end of last row. Work pattern as charted, stopping at armholes, picking up new yarn, and binding off and decreasing as indicated.

SLEEVES: With size 7 needles, cast on 25 sts. Work in rib as for body for 11 rows, increasing 9 sts in the last row—34 sts. Work pattern as charted and bind off loosely.

BUTTON BANDS: Button border: left front for girls, right front for boys. Work 4 rows of single crochet along the front edge. Buttonhole border: right front for girls, left front for boys. Work 2 rows of single crochet along the front edge. In the 3rd row make 4 evenly spaced buttonholes to fit buttons. Crochet one more row.

Sew shoulder seams.

COLLAR: Pick up 32 sts around neck, omitting the button and buttonhole bands. Work 22 rows in Moss stitch. Break off yarn. With another needle and starting from the neck edge pick up 11 sts on the right side of the collar. Work across 32 sts on needle, then pick up 11 sts on the left side. Work a further 4 rows in Moss stitch, then 3 rows in Garter stitch. Bind off loosely.

Sew in sleeves. Join sleeve seams. Sew on buttons.

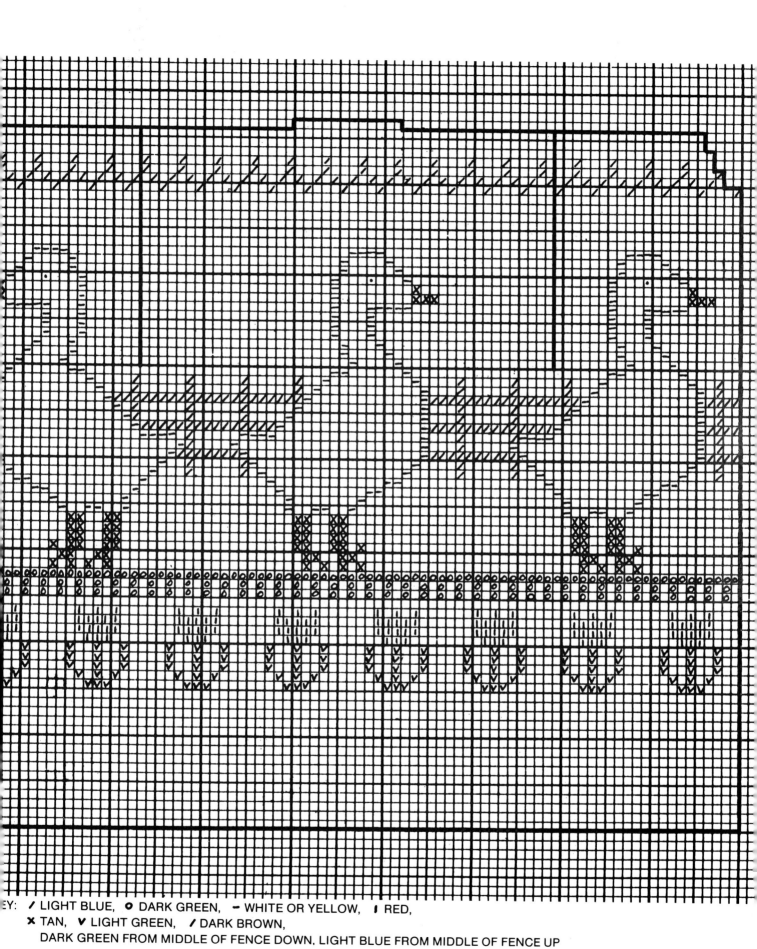

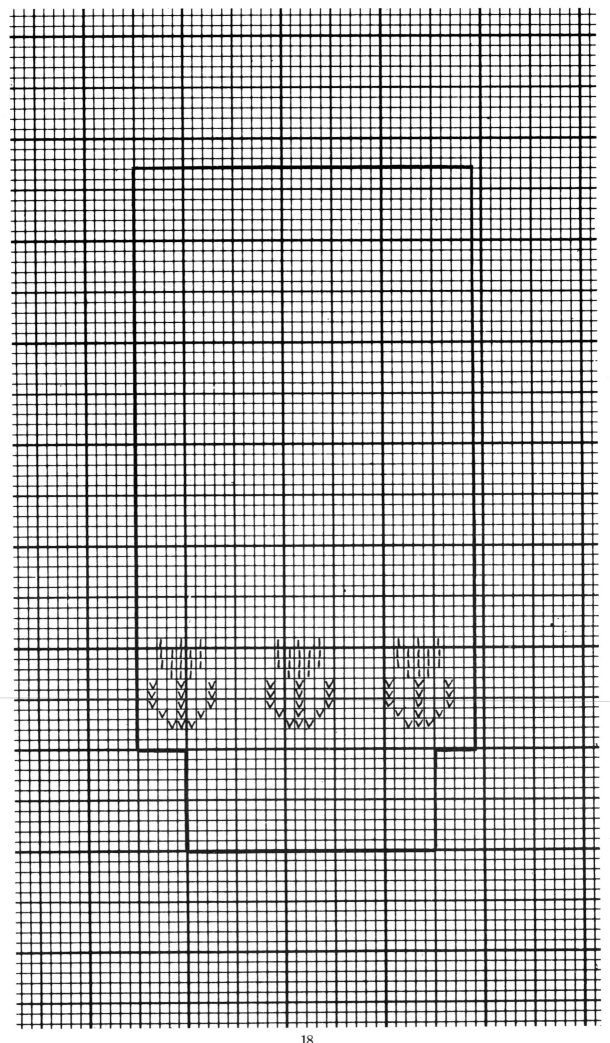

Buckingham Palace Guards
Crew-Neck Pullover

BUCKINGHAM PALACE GUARDS CREW-NECK PULLOVER

Inspired by the famous guards at Buckingham Palace in London, this design is perfect for a small boy. Colorful in red, white, and blue, this is an English must!

MATERIALS: 4 oz. (5 oz., 6 oz., 7 oz.) white in fingering-weight yarn. 2 to 3 oz. of red and 2 to 3 oz. of blue. Small amount of black.

NEEDLES: Size 1 and 3. One set of double-point needles, size 2.

GAUGE: 7 sts = 1 inch; 19 rows = 2 inches.

SIZE: These directions are for a size 2. Changes for size 4, 6, and 8 are in parentheses. Finished chest measurement of sweater is 22 (24, 26, 28) inches.

To alter size see instructions for SIZING.

NOTE: This sweater may be made with thicker yarn and larger needles. A sport-weight yarn worked on size 3 and 5 needles will yield 6 sts to the inch and 7 rows to the inch. Finished chest sizes for the four outlines are 26 (28, 30, 32) inches.

FRONT: With size 1 needles and blue yarn, cast on 78 (84, 88, 96) sts. Work in K2, P2, ribbing for 1¾ (1¾, 2, 2) inches. Change to size 3 needles and K the first row increasing to 80 (86, 92, 98) sts at even intervals. Continue in st st and work the charted design, binding off and decreasing as indicated. Place 22 (24, 26, 26) sts in center front on holder to be picked up for neck.

BACK: Work back to match front keeping blue at bottom and red at top, with red shoulders matching and blue matching at sides. Omit the neck opening, bind off shoulders as indicated and place the center 30 (30, 32, 32) sts on a holder for neck.

SLEEVES: Work one sleeve blue and one sleeve red. With size 1 needles, cast on 36 (36, 40, 40) sts and work ribbing of K2, P2 for 2 (2, 2½, 3) inches. Change to size 3 needles and main color and K across the row increasing to 44 (45, 45, 49) sts at even intervals. P back, then work in st st, increasing 1 st each end of the 7th row, then at each end of every 8th row until there are 61 (63, 67, 73) sts. When the sleeve measures 10 (10¾, 12½, 14) sts from the beginning, ending with a purl row, bind off 5 (5, 5, 6) sts at the beginning of each of the next 2 rows. Then bind off 1 st at the beginning of every row until 31 sts remain. Then 3 sts at the beginning of the next 4 rows. Bind off remaining 19 sts.

Sew shoulder seams.

NECK:　　　　With size 2 double-point needles, and contrasting ribbing color, pick up 88 (88, 92, 96) sts, including those on stitch holders around the neck. Work in K2, P2 ribbing for 8 rows. Bind off loosely in ribbing pattern on next row.

An alternative neck opening is to leave one shoulder seam half way open. Single-edge crochet around both sides of open half, add single crochet buttonholes and add buttons.

Sew sleeves in place. Sew underarm and sleeve seams. Weave in loose threads.

Rag-Rug Vest

RAG-RUG VEST

Just as in the old rag carpets that were made from randomly woven scraps of fabric, this little vest is a derivative, using lots of varied color yarns (and varied textures too, if you'd like) and knitting them into a copy of a mid-19th-century rag carpet. The stripes up each side simulate suspenders. The trick in this easy-to-knit sweater is to make the stripes very random, starting and stopping them in different places and widening and thinning the horizontal stripes.

MATERIALS: 1 oz. of color for vertical stripes. 1 oz. of color for ribbing. 2 to 3 oz. of miscellaneous colors for stripes. Yarn used should be sport-weight, Shetland, or yarn recommended for gauge below.

NEEDLES: Size 3 and 5. One set of double-point needles, size 3.

GAUGE: 6 sts = 1 inch; 7–7½ rows = 1 inch.

SIZE: These directions are for a size 1. Changes for sizes 2 and 4 are given in parentheses. Finished chest measurement of sweater is 19½ (21½, 23½) inches.

NOTE: This sweater may be made with thicker yarn and larger needles. A heavier sport-weight, cotton, or 2-ply worsted yarn worked on size 4 and 6 needles with a gauge of 5 sts to the inch and 6 rows to the inch, will give finished chest sizes of 23 (25½, 28) inches.

FRONT: With size 3 needles, cast on 54 (60, 66) sts. Work in K1, P1, ribbing for 1½ inches. Change to size 5 needles and working in st st increase 4 sts evenly spaced across first row. Using the chart, knit random rows of horizontal color, stopping and starting in different places and varying the size of the stripes, and at the same time running rows of a contrasting color vertically for stripes. (These may also be added after the sweater is completed using a chain stitch on the right side of the sweater.) Stripes running vertically should start 2 or 3 sts from neck edge.

BACK: Work back to match front. Use upper line of graph for back neck opening. Place the center 16 sts on a holder for neck ribbing.

Sew shoulder and side seams, leaving one shoulder partly opened if buttons are desired.

NECK: With size 3 double-point needles, and right side facing, pick up 48 sts including sts on front and back holders and work in K1, P1, ribbing for ¾ inch, leaving side and shoulder open for button closure. Bind off loosely in K1, P1, ribbing. Single-edge crochet around both sides of open section of neck and shoulder. Add single-crochet buttonholes and buttons.

ARMHOLES: With size 3 double-point needles, and right side facing, pick up 56 (62, 62) sts and work in K1, P1, ribbing for ¾ inch. Bind off loosely in ribbing.

Weave in loose threads from pattern work.

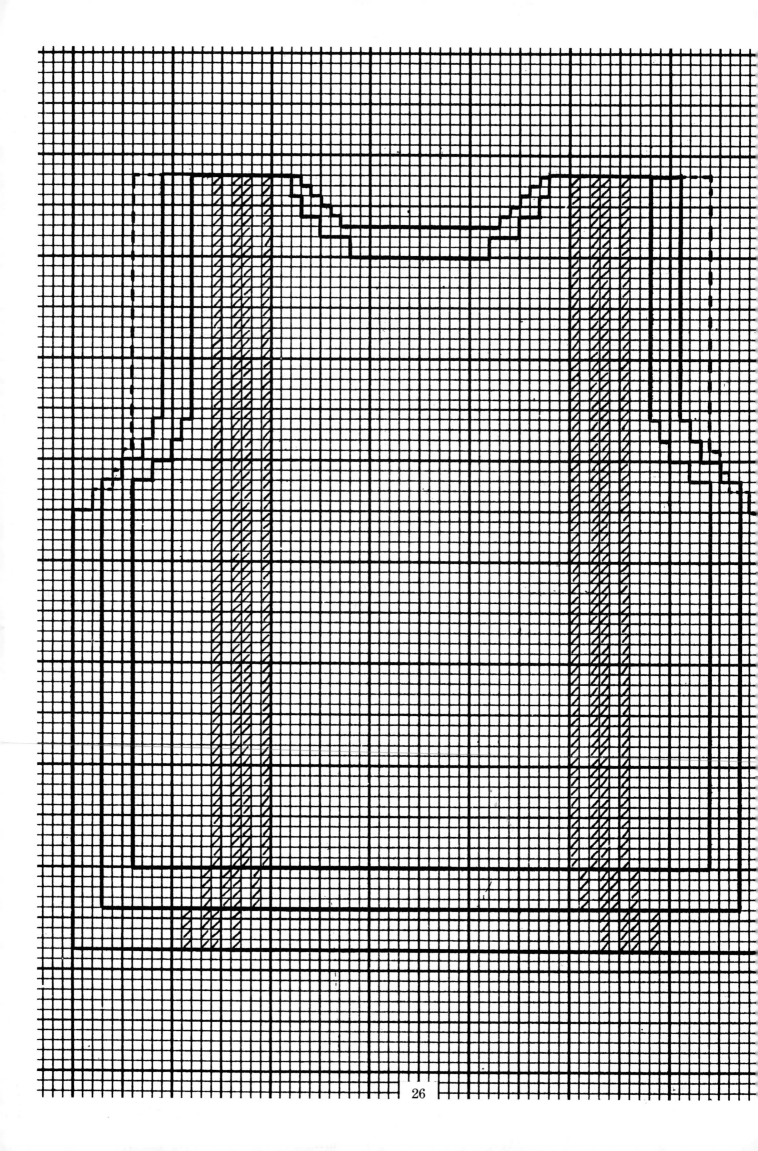

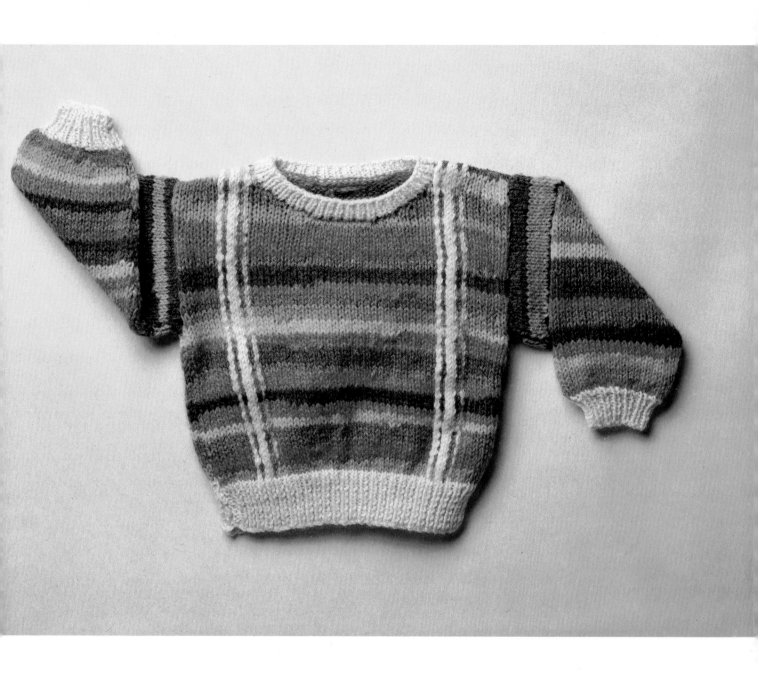

Rag-Rug Crew-Neck Pullover

RAG-RUG CREW-NECK PULLOVER

The rag-rug looks just as good as a pullover as it does as a vest. Make the stripes very random and stop and start at different places for a really old 19th-century carpet effect.

MATERIALS: 6 oz. (7 oz., 8 oz., 9 oz.) random colors in fingering-weight yarn. Dark color for stripes up side.

NEEDLES: Size 1 and 3. One set of double-point needles, size 2.

GAUGE: 7 sts = 1 inch; 19 rows = 2 inches.

SIZE: These directions are for a size 2. Changes for size 4, 6, and 8 are given in parentheses. Finished chest measurement of sweater is 22 (24, 26, 28) inches.

To alter size see instructions for SIZING.

NOTE: This sweater may be made with thicker yarn and larger needles. A sport-weight yarn worked on size 3 and 5 needles will yield 6 sts to the inch and 7 rows to the inch. Finished chest sizes for the four outlines are 26 (28, 30, 32) inches.

FRONT: With size 1 needles, and contrasting ribbing color, cast on 78 (84, 88, 96) sts. Work in K2, P2, ribbing for 1¾ (1¾, 2, 2) inches. Change to size 3 needles and main color and K the first row increasing to 80 (86, 92, 98) sts at even intervals. Continue in st st and work the charted design, binding off and decreasing as indicated. Place 22 (24, 26, 26) sts in center front on holder to be picked up for neck.

BACK: Work back to match front. Omit the neck opening, bind off shoulders as indicated and place and center 30 (30, 32, 32) sts on a holder for neck.

SLEEVES: With size 1 needles, and contrasting ribbing color, cast on 36 (36, 40, 40) sts and work ribbing of K2, P2 for 2 (2, 2½, 3) inches. Change to size 3 needles and main color and K across the row increasing to 44 (45, 45, 49) sts at even intervals. P back, then work in st st, increasing 1 st each end of the 7th row, then at each end of every 8th row until there are 61 (63, 67, 73) sts. When the sleeve measures 10 (10¾, 12½, 14) sts from the beginning, ending with a purl row, bind off 5 (5, 5, 6) sts at the beginning of each of the next 2 rows. Then bind off 1 st at beginning of every row until 31 sts remain. Then 3 sts at the beginning of the next 4 rows. Bind off remaining 19 sts.

Sew shoulder seams.

NECK: With size 2 double-point needles, and contrasting ribbing color, pick up 88 (88, 92, 96) sts, including those on stitch holders around the neck. Work in K2, P2 ribbing for 8 rows. Bind off loosely in ribbing pattern on next row.

An alternative neck opening is to leave one shoulder seam half way open. Single-edge crochet around both sides of open half, add single-crochet buttonholes and add buttons.

Sew sleeves in place. Sew underarm and sleeve seams. Weave in loose threads.

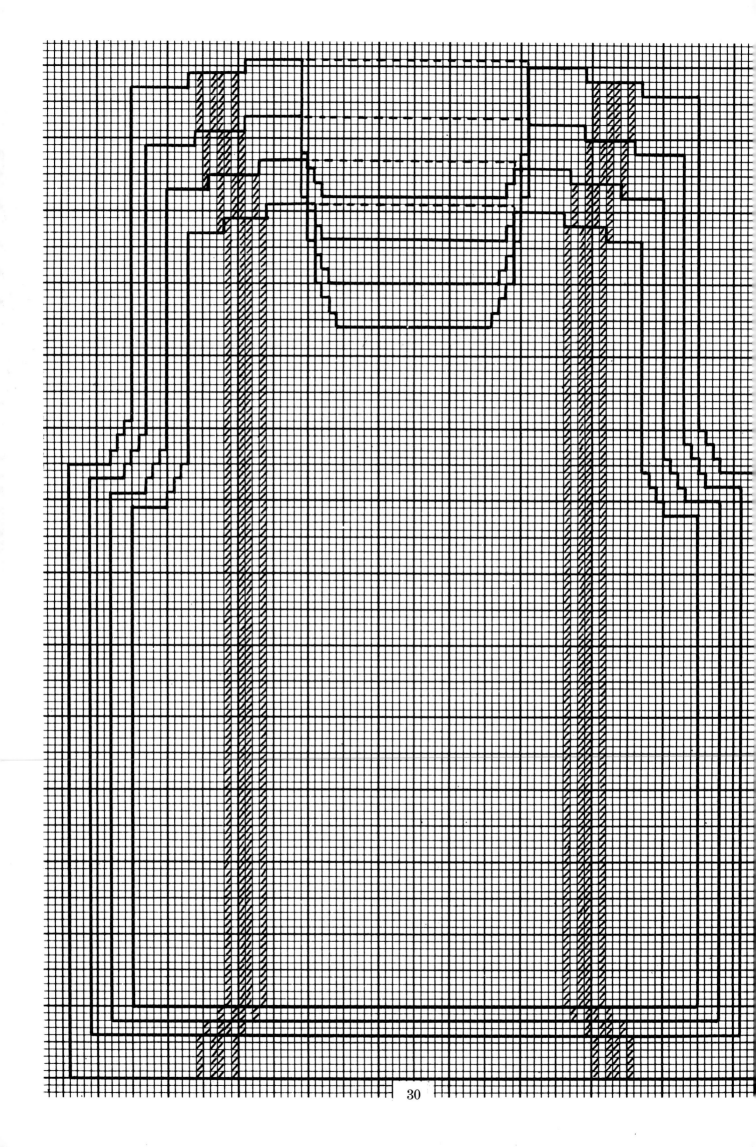

Rockinghorse Vest

ROCKINGHORSE VEST

A mid-19th-century rocking horse looks great worked up as a child's vest. We designed it originally for a friend who owns a shop by the same name. Kids love it and different color combinations are fun and creative. We have worked up a couple with striped backgrounds and windowpane checks.

MATERIALS: 3 to 4 oz. of main color in sport-weight, Shetland, or yarn recommended for gauge below. Small amounts of five different colors for pattern.

NEEDLES: Size 3 and 5. One set of double-point needles, size 3.

GAUGE: 6 sts = 1 inch; 7–7½ rows = 1 inch.

SIZE: These directions are for a size 1. Changes for sizes 2 and 4 are given in parentheses. Finished chest measurement of sweater is 19½ (21½, 23½) inches.

NOTE: This sweater may be made with thicker yarn and larger needles. A heavier sport-weight, cotton, or 2-ply worsted yarn worked on size 4 and 6 needles with a gauge of 5 sts to the inch and 6 rows to the inch will give finished chest sizes of 23 (25½, 28) inches.

FRONT: With size 3 needles, cast on 54 (60, 66) sts. Work K1, P1, ribbing for 1½ inches. Change to size 5 needles and working in st st increase 4 sts evenly spaced across first row. Continue in st st and work the charted design, binding off and decreasing as indicated. Place the 14 sts in center of front on holder to be picked up later for neck ribbing.

BACK: Work back to match front. Use upper line of graph for back neck opening. Place the center 16 sts on a holder for neck ribbing.

Sew shoulder and side seams, leaving one shoulder partly opened if buttons are desired.

NECK: With size 3 double-point needles, and right side facing, pick up 48 sts including sts on front and back holders and work in K1, P1, ribbing for ¾ inch, leaving side and shoulder open for button closure. Bind off loosely in K1, P1, ribbing. Single-edge crochet around both sides of open section of neck and shoulder. Add single-edge crochet buttonholes and buttons.

ARMHOLES: With size 3 double-point needles, and right side facing, pick up 56 (62, 62) sts and work in K1, P1, ribbing for ¾ inch. Bind off loosely in ribbing.

Weave in loose threads from pattern work. Swiss-darn eye on horse.

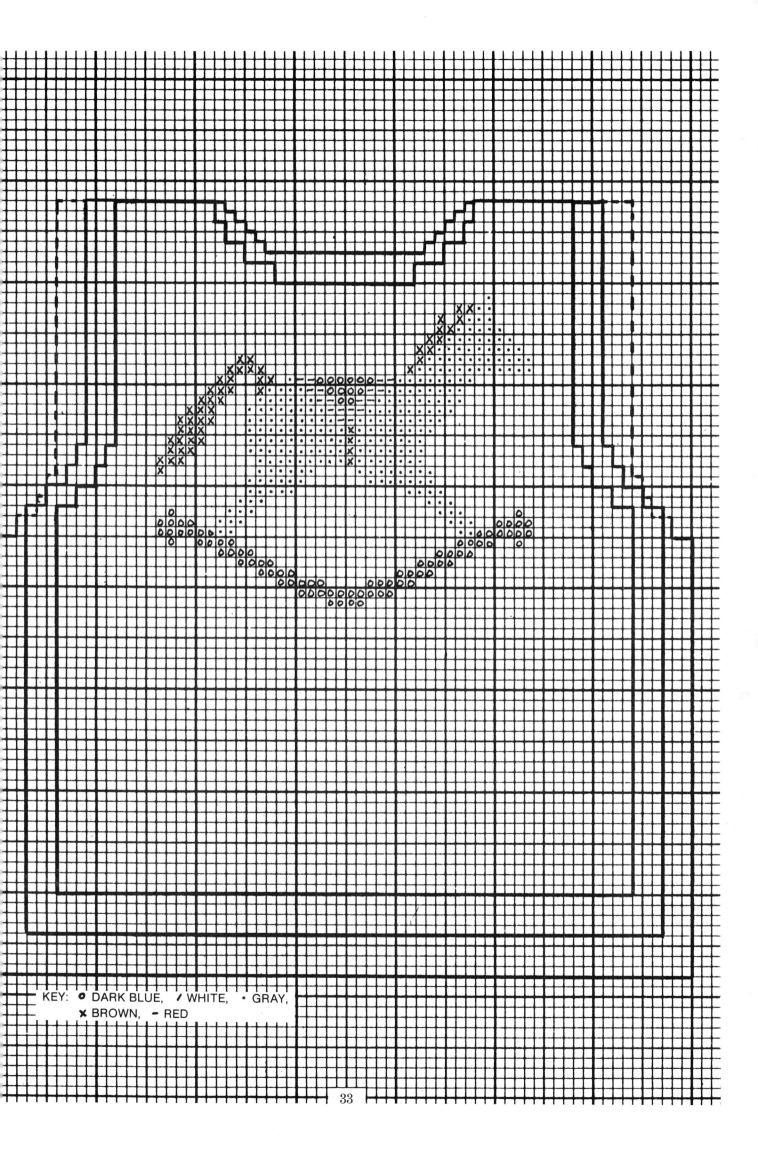

KEY: **o** DARK BLUE, **/** WHITE, **·** GRAY,
x BROWN, **-** RED

Patchwork Vest

PATCHWORK VEST

A sampler patchwork, with lots of different squares. It is based on old quilts made from scraps and given to a young girl to practice with. It is a good way to use up oddments and is a colorful and fun addition to a youngster's wardrobe.

MATERIALS: 2 oz. of 4 different colors in sport-weight, Shetland, or yarn recommended for gauge below.

NEEDLES: Size 3 and 5. One set of double-point needles, size 3.

GAUGE: 6 sts = 1 inch; 7–7½ rows = 1 inch.

SIZE: These directions are for a size 1. Changes for sizes 2 and 4 are given in parentheses. Finished chest measurement of sweater is 19½ (21½, 23½) inches.

NOTE: This sweater may be made with thicker yarn and larger needles. A heavier sport-weight, cotton, or 2-ply worsted yarn worked on size 4 and 6 needles with a gauge of 5 sts to the inch and 6 rows to the inch will give finished chest sizes of 23 (25½, 28) inches.

FRONT: With size 3 needles, cast on 54 (60, 66) sts. Work in K1, P1, ribbing for 1½ inches. Change to size 5 needles and working in st st increase 4 sts evenly spaced across first row. Continue in st st and work the charted design, binding off and decreasing as indicated. Place the 14 sts in center of front on holder to be picked up later for neck ribbing.

BACK: Work back to match front. Use upper line of graph for back neck opening. Place the center 16 sts on a holder for neck ribbing.

Sew shoulder and side seams, leaving one shoulder partly opened if buttons are desired.

NECK: With size 3 double-point needles, and right side facing, pick up 48 sts including sts on front and back holders and work in K1, P1, ribbing for ¾ inch, leaving side and shoulder open for button closure. Bind off loosely in K1, P1, ribbing. Single-edge crochet around both sides of open section of neck and shoulder. Add single-edge crochet buttonholes and buttons.

ARMHOLES: With size 3 double-point needles, and right side facing, pick up 56 (62, 62) sts and work in K1, P1, ribbing for ¾ inch. Bind off loosely in ribbing.

Weave in loose threads from pattern work.

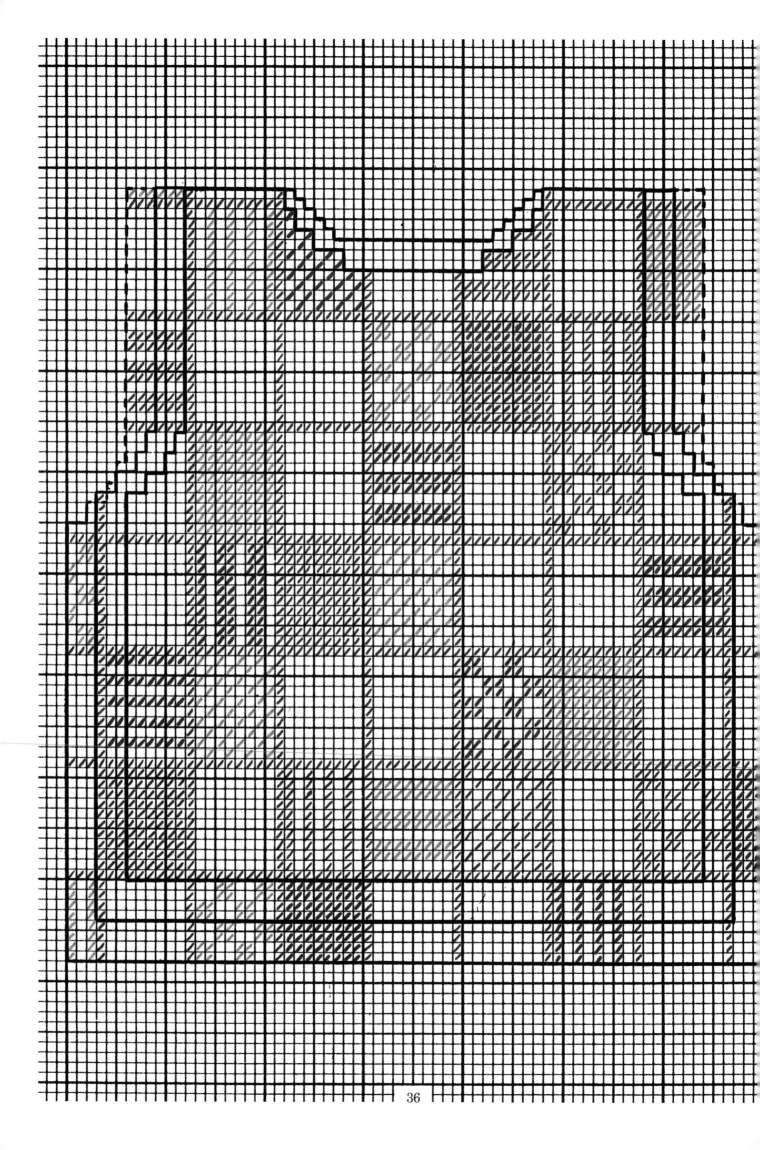

Ship Crew-Neck Pullover

SHIP CREW-NECK PULLOVER

A big sailing vessel is the central motif for this quick and easy-to-knit sweater. Red, white, and blue are the traditional colors and make the sweater a favorite for boys.

MATERIALS: 8 to 10 oz. of main color in featherweight knitting worsted, Shetland, sport-weight, or other yarn recommended to give gauge below. 3 oz. of white. Small amounts of dark brown and color to outline sails.

NEEDLES: Size 3 and 4. One set of double-point needles, size 3.

GAUGE: 6½ sts = 1 inch; 8 rows = 1 inch.

SIZE: These directions are for a size 8 with a finished chest measurement of 28½ inches.

To alter size see instructions for SIZING.

FRONT: With main color and size 3 needles cast on 88 sts. Work in K1, P1, ribbing for 2 inches. Change to larger needles and increase 6 sts in next row working in st st. Follow graph. Decrease and bind off as indicated and place center sts on holder for neck.

BACK: Work as for front, omitting ship, but continuing on with stripes.

SLEEVES: With smaller needles cast on 50 sts. Work in K1, P1, ribbing for 1½ inches. Change to larger needles and increase 8 sts evenly spaced on next row working in st st. Follow graph. Increase and bind off as indicated. Bind off loosely.

Sew shoulder seams.

NECK: With double-point needles, pick up 94 sts around neck edge and work in K1, P1, ribbing for 5 rows. Bind off loosely in ribbing.

Sew side and underarm seams. Work in loose threads.

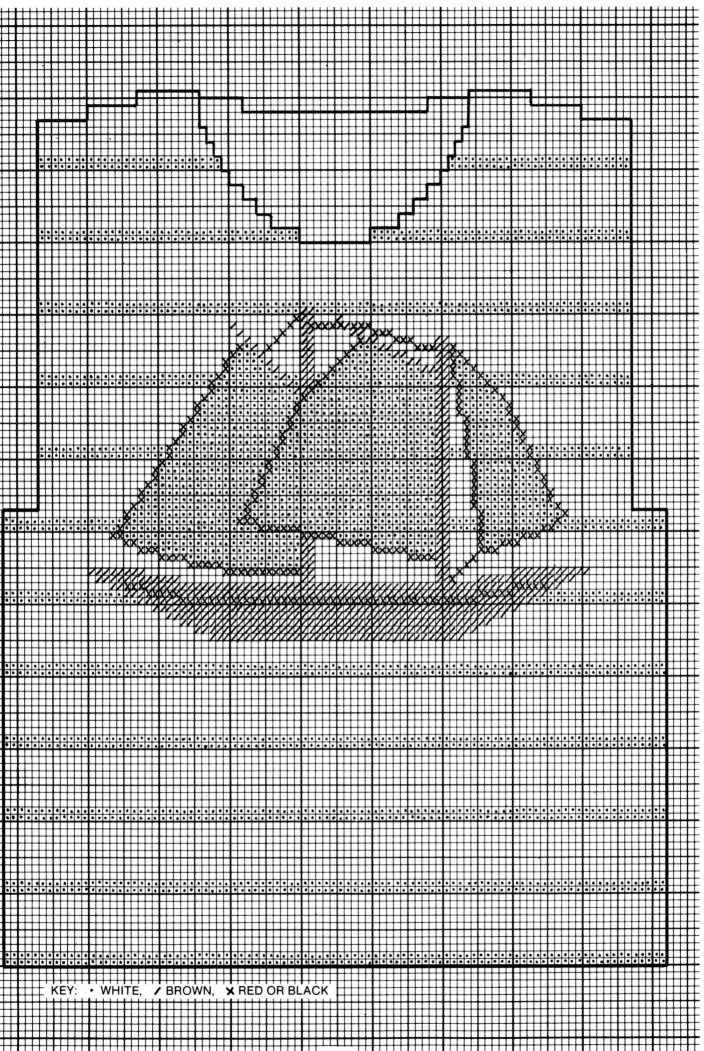

KEY: • WHITE, ╱ BROWN, ✖ RED OR BLACK

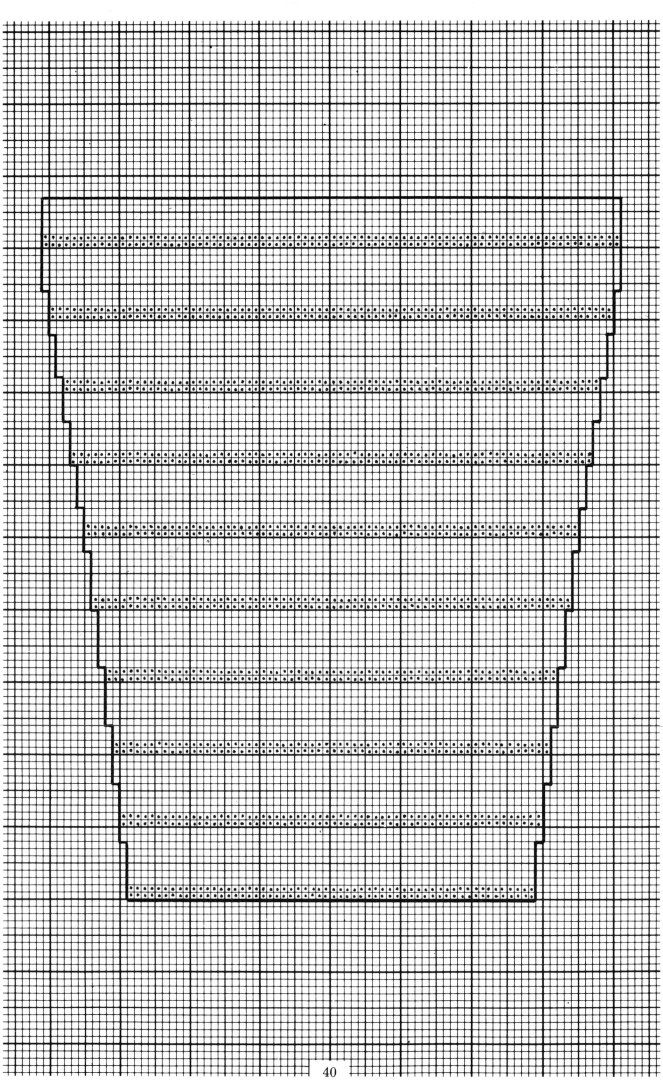

Rabbit Crew-Neck Pullover

RABBIT CREW-NECK PULLOVER I

A wonderful rendition of a lovable bunny hopping right out of his framed boundary into a field of pink flowers. He's a BIG hit wherever he goes. On an off-white ground, he can be knit as a white-and-black fluffy rabbit, or a more subtle gray-and-black wool rabbit. Flowers are knit with entire circles filled in, or for an open and interesting look, leave the center white and make the circles with pink. No matter which you choose, he'll fast become a favorite.

MATERIALS: 4 to 6 oz. of background color in fingering-weight yarn. 2 oz. dark green for leaves and stems. 2 oz. pink for flowers and frame. 1 oz. light green for background color inside frame. 1 oz. white angora, mohair, bouclé, or wool for rabbit. 1 oz. black or dark gray angora, mohair, bouclé, or wool for rabbit.

NEEDLES: Size 1 and 3. One set double-point needles, size 2.

GAUGE: 7 sts = 1 inch; 19 rows = 2 inches.

SIZE: These directions are for a size 2. Changes for sizes 4, 6, and 8 are in parentheses. Finished chest measurement of sweater is 22 (24, 26, 28) inches.

To alter size see instructions for SIZING.

NOTE: This sweater may be made with thicker yarn and larger needles. A sport-weight yarn worked on size 3 and 5 needles will give 6 sts to the inch and 7 rows to the inch. Finished garment will have a chest measurement of 25 inches.

FRONT: With size 1 needles, and main color, cast on 72 (84, 88, 96) sts. Work in K2, P2, ribbing for 1¾ (1¾, 2, 2) inches. Change to size 3 needles and increase at intervals to make 76 (86, 92, 98) sts, working in st st. Continue in st st and follow charted design. Increase, decrease and bind off as indicated. Place center sts 16 (20, 22, 25) on holder for neck.

BACK: Work to match front, using chart for back design.

SLEEVES: With size 1 needles and main color, cast on 46 (46, 48, 48) sts and work in ribbing of K2, P2 for 2 (2, 2½, 3) inches. Change to size 3 needles and knit across row in st st increasing to 50 (50, 52, 52) sts. Follow chart for sleeves, increasing and binding off as indicated.

Sew shoulder seams.

NECK: With size 2 double-point needles, and main color, pick up 88 (88, 92, 96) sts, including those on st holders around neck. Work in K2, P2, ribbing for 8 rows. Bind off loosely in ribbing.

An alternative neck opening is to leave one shoulder seam half way open. Single-edge crochet around both sides of open half, add single-crochet buttonholes and add buttons.

Sew sleeves in place. Sew underarm and sleeve seams. Weave in loose threads.

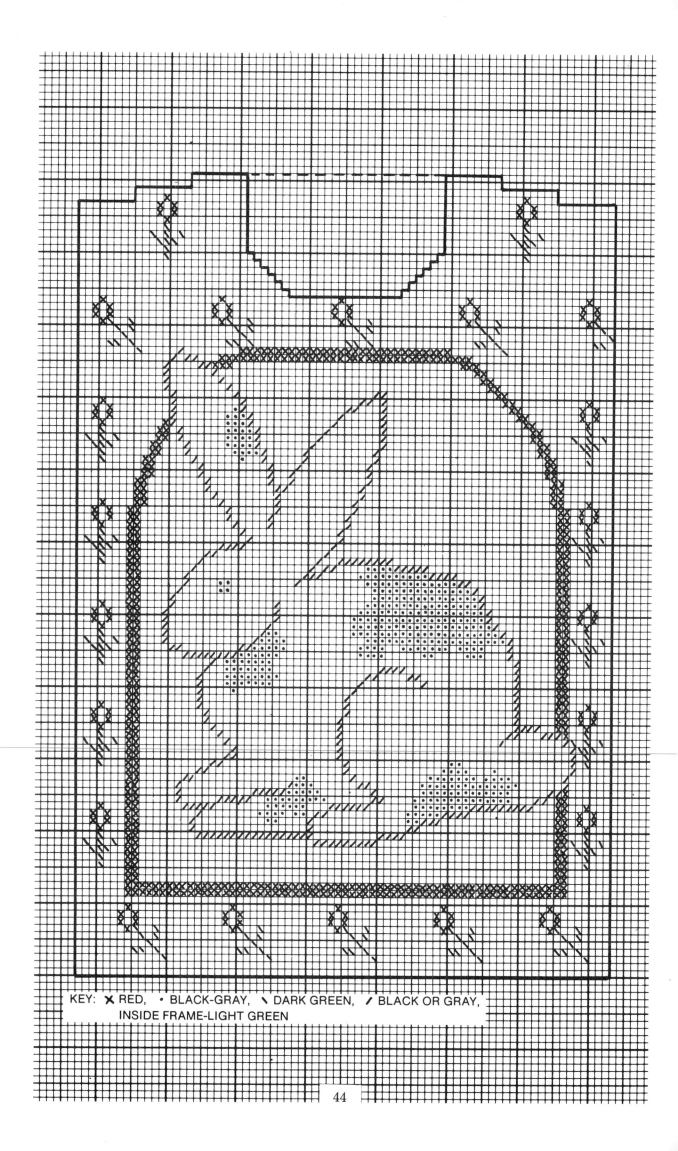

KEY: ✗ RED, • BLACK-GRAY, ＼ DARK GREEN, ／ BLACK OR GRAY,
INSIDE FRAME-LIGHT GREEN

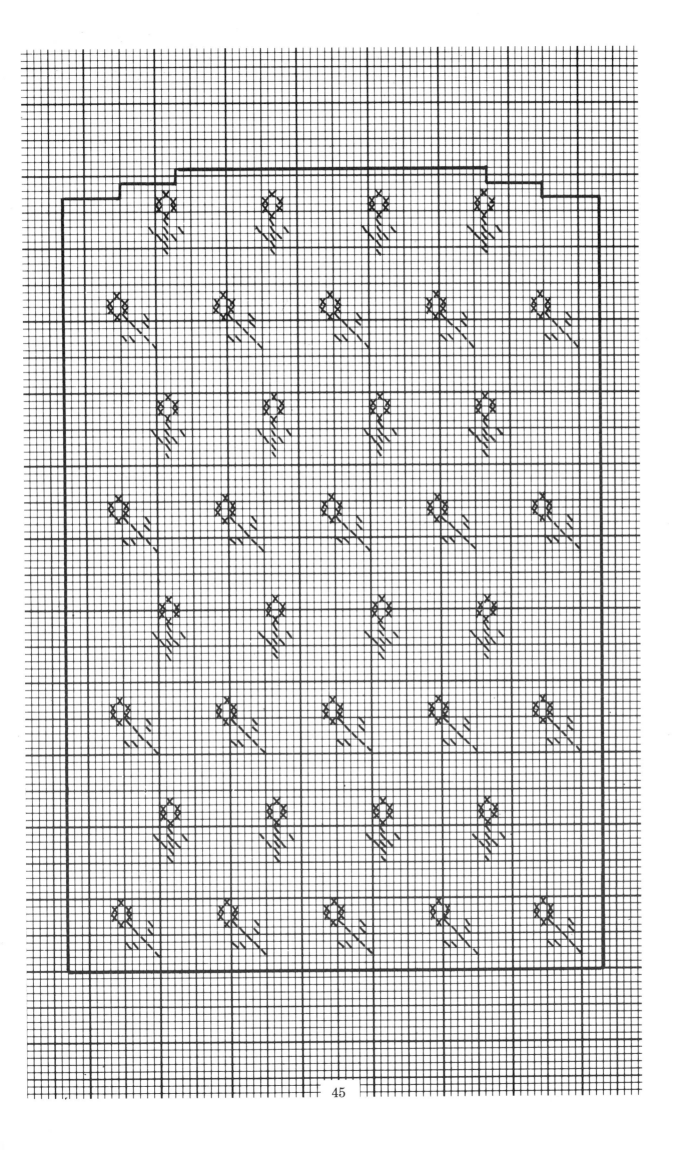

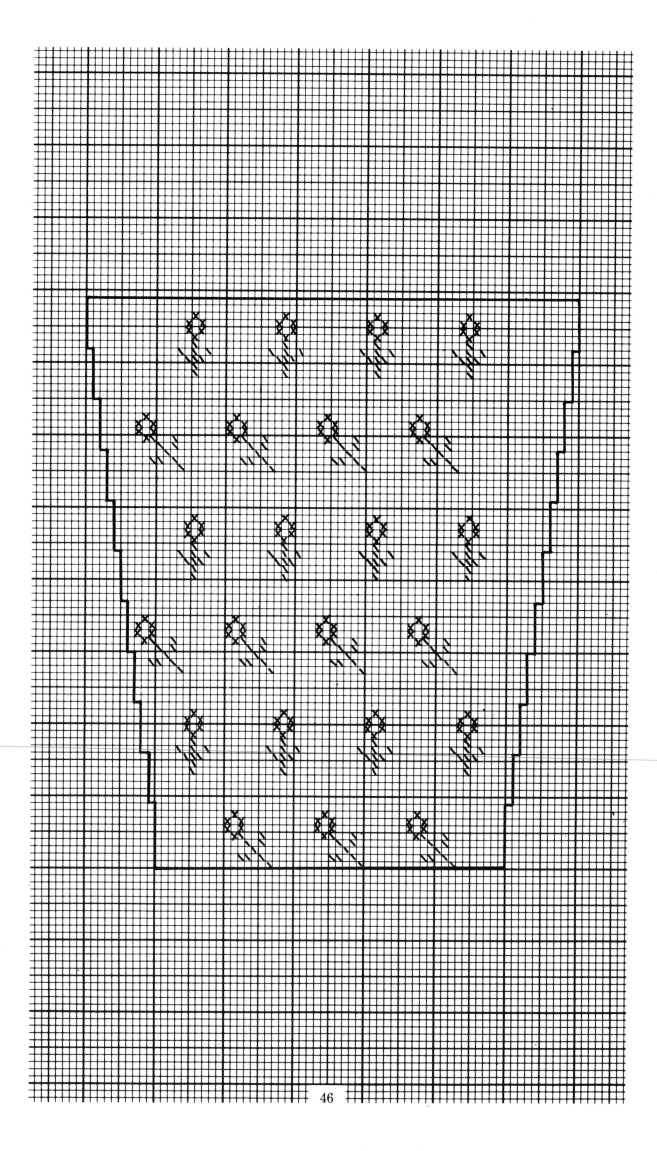

RABBIT CREW-NECK PULLOVER II

This second version of our Bunny design uses the same motif and works up into a larger size. These directions are for a size 8 (oversize) sweater.

MATERIALS: 12 to 15 oz. of background color in fingering-weight yarn. 2 oz. dark green for leaves and stems. 2 oz. pink for flowers and frame. 1 oz. light green for background color inside frame. 2 oz. white angora, mohair, bouclé, or wool for rabbit. 1 oz. black and dark gray angora, mohair, bouclé, or wool for rabbit.

NEEDLES: Size 1 and 3. One set double-point needles, size 2.

GAUGE: 7 sts = 1 inch; 8½–9 rows = inch.

SIZE: These directions are for a size 8 (oversize) sweater. Finished chest measurement is 31½ inches.

To alter size see instructions for SIZING.

NOTE: This sweater may be made with thicker yarn and larger needles. A sport-weight yarn worked on size 3 and 5 needles will give 6 sts to the inch and 7 rows to the inch. Finished chest measurement is 36½ inches.

FRONT: With smaller needles cast on 98 sts and work in K2, P2, ribbing for 2½ inches. Change to larger needles and increase 12 sts evenly spaced across next row working in st st. Continue in st st and work charted design binding off as indicated. Place center sts on holder for neck.

BACK: Work back to match front, omitting bunny pattern and working flowers as diagramed. Place center sts on holder for neck.

SLEEVES: With smaller needles cast on 40 sts and work in K2, P2, ribbing for 3 inches. Change to larger needles and increase 36 sts evenly spaced in next row working in st st. Continue in st st and work sleeves according to charted design. Bind off loosely.

Sew shoulder seams.

NECK: With double-point needles, pick up a total of 104 sts, including sts from front and back holders. Work in K1, P1, ribbing for 1 inch. Bind off loosely.

Sew sleeves in place. Sew underarm and sleeve seams. Weave in loose threads.

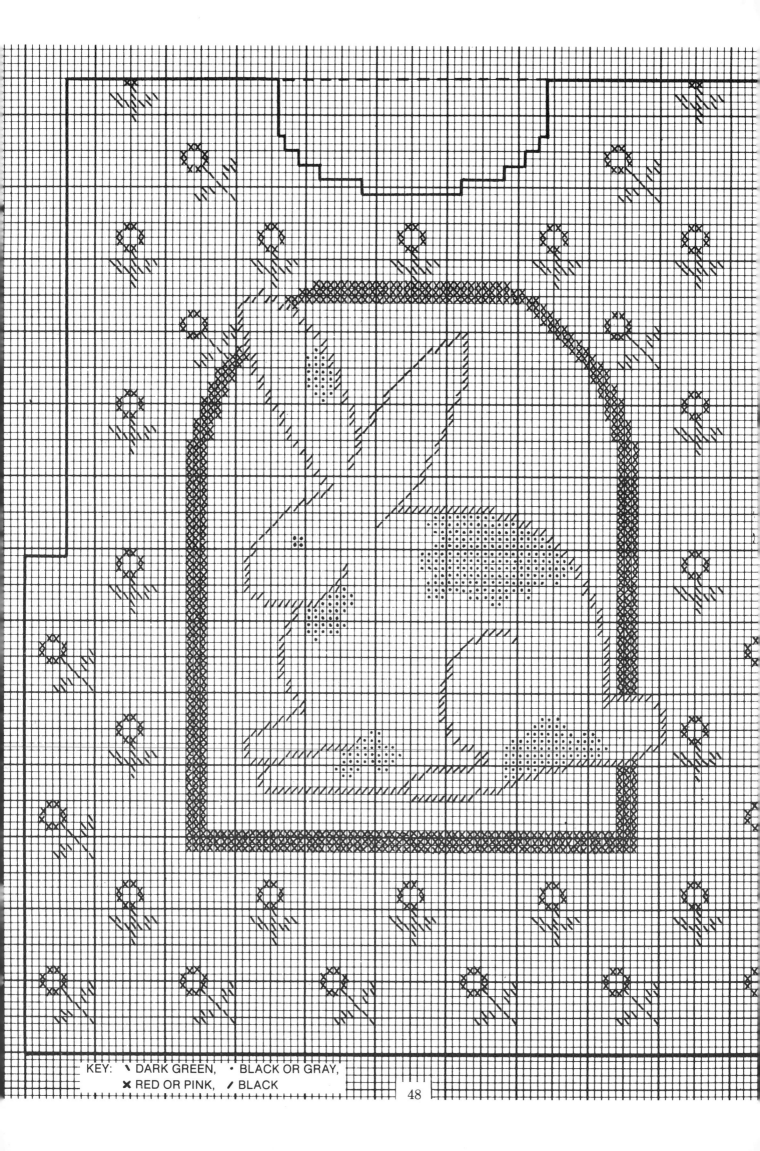

KEY: ⟍ DARK GREEN,   • BLACK OR GRAY,
        ✗ RED OR PINK,   ╱ BLACK

48

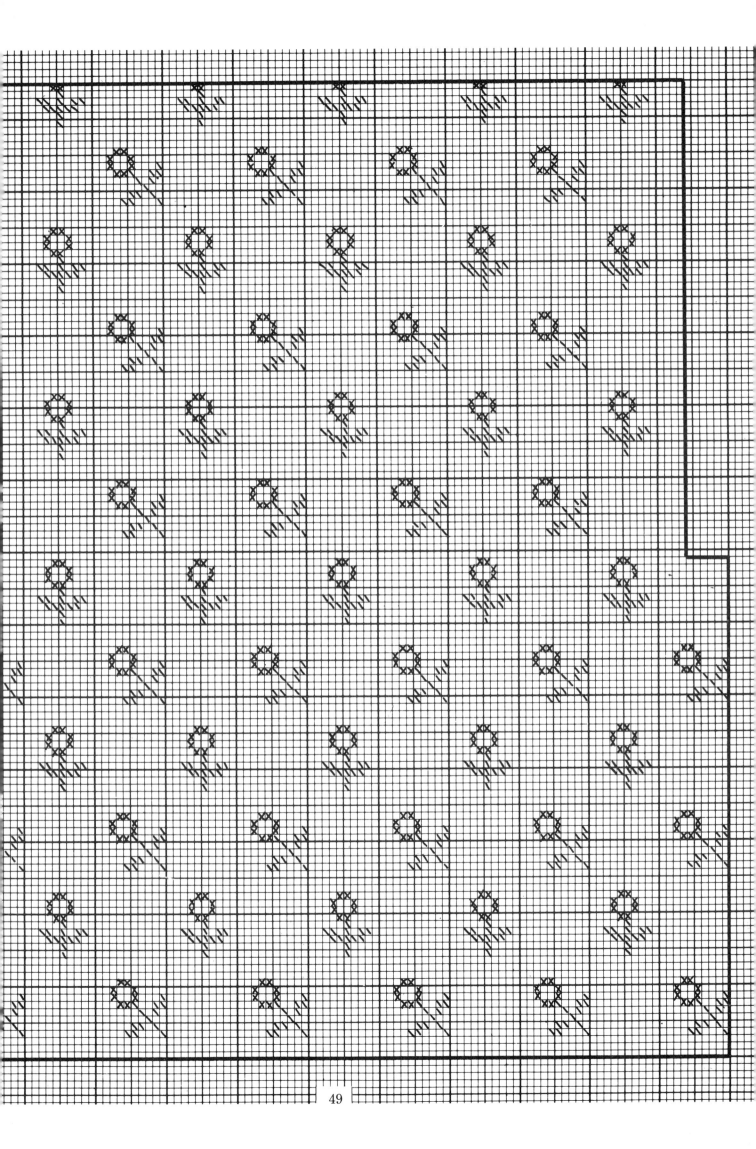

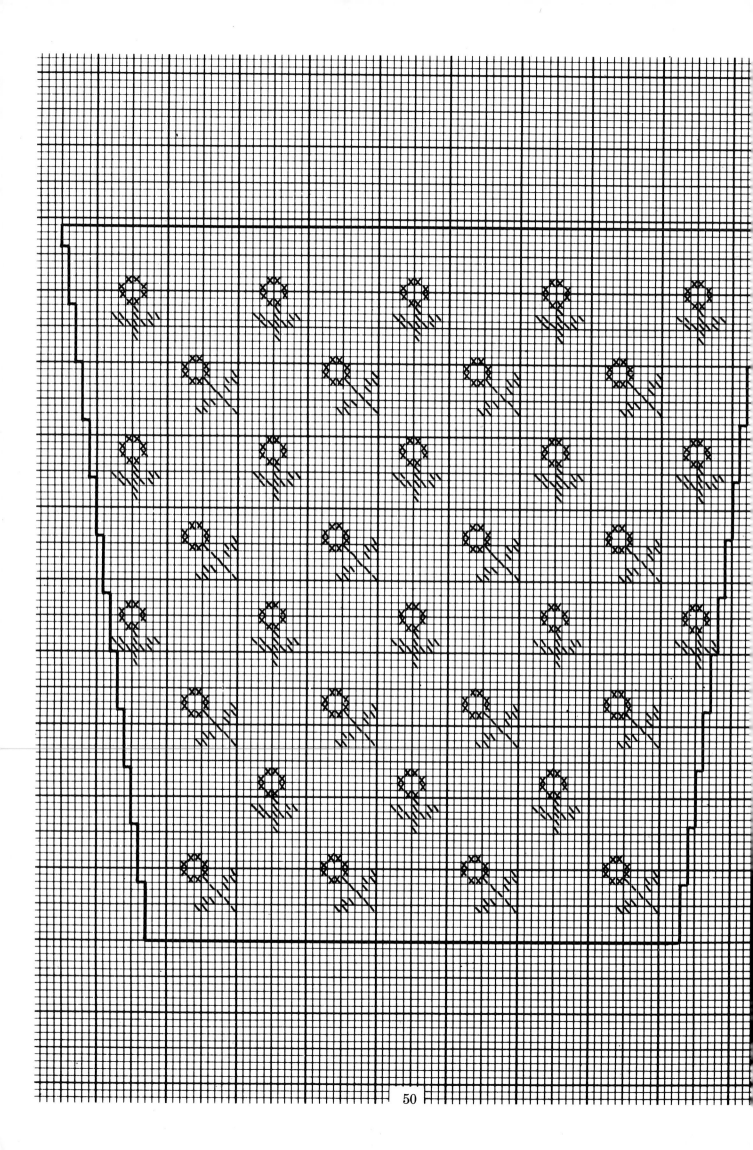

Basket Quilt Crew-Neck Pullover

BASKET QUILT CREW-NECK PULLOVER

This version of the Basket Quilt Pullover is designed for sizes 8 to 14. It can also be adapted to a cardigan by following the graph for the basket and directions for the Country Goose Cardigan (page 64).

MATERIALS: 12 to 15 oz. background color in featherweight knitting worsted, Shetland, sport-weight, or other yarn recommended for gauge below. 2 to 3 oz. color for diamonds. 2 to 3 oz. each of two colors for basket.

NEEDLES: Size 3 and 5. One set of double-point needles, size 3.

GAUGE: 6 sts = 1 inch; 7½ rows = 1 inch using size 5 needles.

SIZE: These directions are for a size 10 30-inch finished garment. Measurements are as follows: length to underarm 13 inches, length to shoulder 20 inches, length of sleeve to underarm 15½ inches.

To alter size see instructions for SIZING.

FRONT: With size 3 needles, cast on 80 sts. Work in K1, P1, ribbing for 3 inches. Change to size 5 needles and increase 8 sts evenly spaced on next row, working in st st. Continue in st st and work the charted design, binding off and decreasing as indicated. Place 14 sts in center of front on holder for neck.

BACK: Work back to match front using chart for pattern. Fill in pattern at neck with designs being used and place 26 sts in center of back on holder for neck.

SLEEVES: Cast on 40 sts on size 3 needles and work in ribbing K1, P1, for 3 inches. Change to size 5 needles and increase 8 sts evenly spaced in next row using st st. Work sleeves according to charted design.

Sew shoulder seams.

NECK: With size 3 double-point needles, K across sts on back holder with right side facing. Pick up and K 56 sts to right shoulder (including sts on front holder). K1, P1, in ribbing on 80 sts for 1 inch. Bind off loosely in ribbing.

Sew sleeves in place. Sew underarm and sleeve seams. Weave in loose threads.

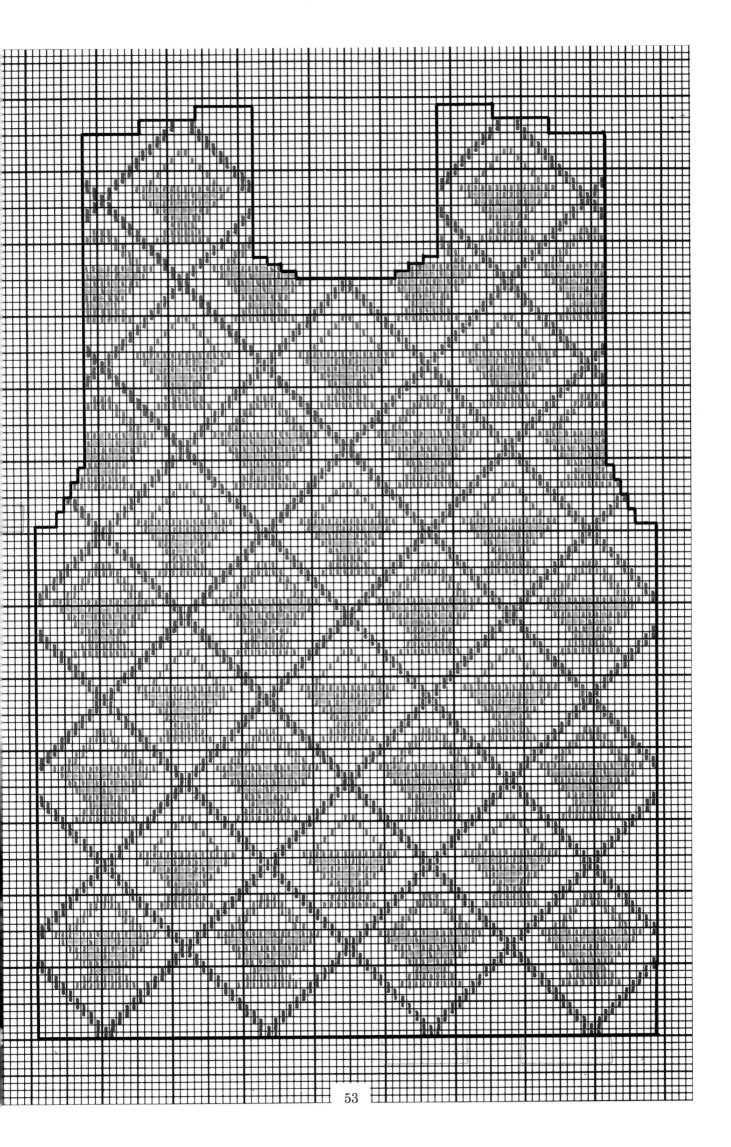

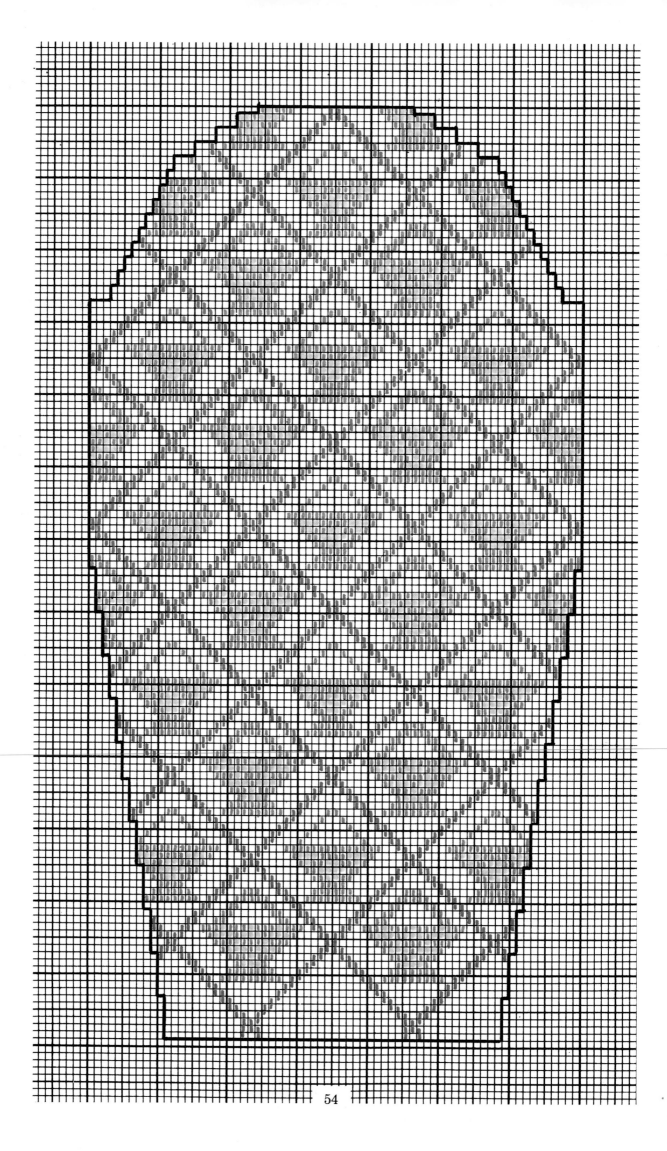

Flying Kites Crew-Neck Pullover

FLYING KITES CREW-NECK PULLOVER

A wonderful sweater for breezy spring days, and what better thing to do than "go fly a kite." It's colorful and happy with a great motif. A perfect sweater for outdoor wear in the spring and fall.

MATERIALS: 4 to 5 oz. light blue for sky in featherweight knitting worsted, Shetland, sport-weight, or other yarn recommended for gauge below. 4 to 5 oz. of green. 2 to 3 oz. of red, black, brown, yellow, white, dark blue, and tan.

NEEDLES: Size 3 and 5. One set of double-point needles, size 3.

GAUGE: 6 sts = 1 inch; 7½ rows = 1 inch, using size 5 needles.

SIZE: These directions are for a size 10 30-inch finished garment. Measurements are as follows: length to underarm 13 inches, length to shoulder 20 inches, length of sleeve to underarm 15½ inches.

To alter size see instructions for SIZING.

FRONT: With size 3 needles, cast on 80 sts. Work in K1, P1, ribbing for 3 inches. Change to size 5 needles and increase 8 sts evenly spaced on next row, working in st st. Continue in st st and work the charted design, binding off and decreasing as indicated. Place 14 sts in center of front on holder for neck.

BACK: Work back to match front using chart for pattern. Fill in pattern at neck with designs being used and place 26 sts in center of back on holder for neck.

SLEEVES: Cast on 40 sts on size 3 needles and work in ribbing K1, P1, for 3 inches. Change to size 5 needles and increase 8 sts evenly spaced in next row using st st. Work sleeves according to charted design.

Sew shoulder seams.

NECK: With size 3 double-point needles, K across sts on back holder with right side facing. Pick up and K 56 sts to right shoulder (including sts on front holder). K1, P1, in ribbing on 80 sts for 1 inch. Bind off loosely in ribbing.

Sew sleeves in place. Sew underarm and sleeve seams. Weave in loose threads. Swiss-darn strings and details on the kites.

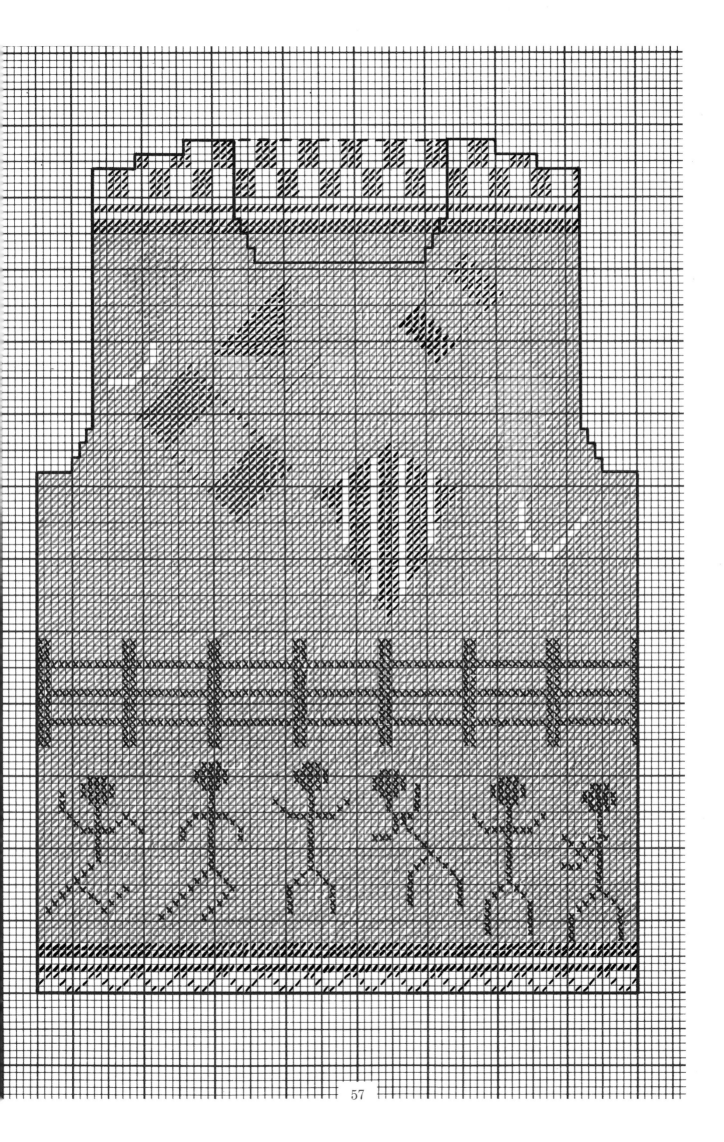

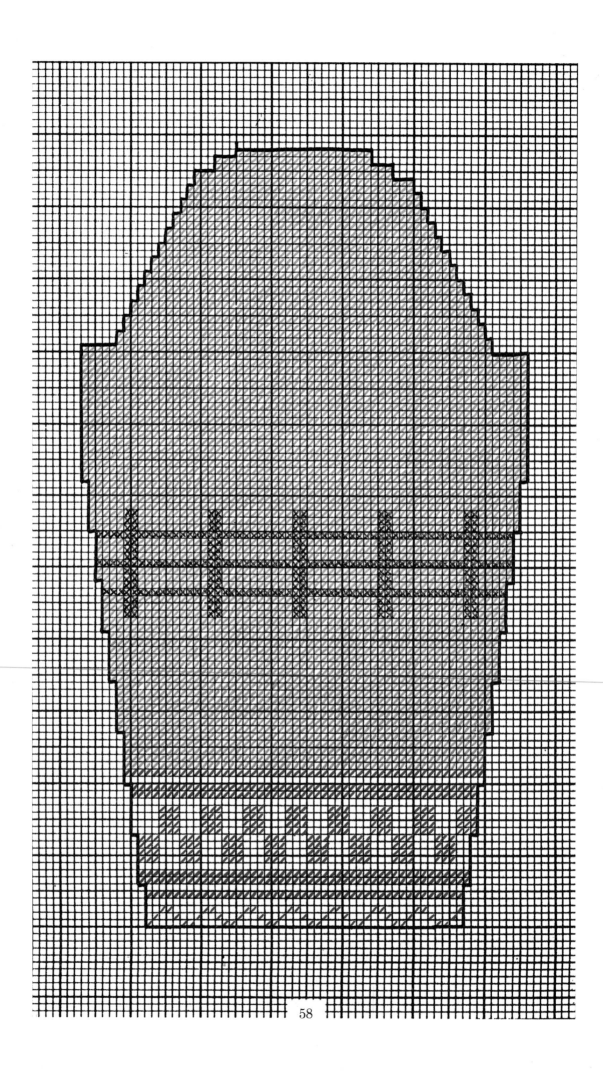

Country Goose Crew-Neck Pullover

COUNTRY GOOSE CREW-NECK PULLOVER

The Country Goose, the most popular of all of our designs, is the one you knitters have many times asked for in a child's version. Here it is for sizes 10 to 14. It makes up into a stunning and ever-popular country classic.

MATERIALS: 12 oz. off-white or other background color in featherweight knitting worsted, Shetland, sport-weight, or other yarn recommended for gauge below. 2½ oz. of dark green, light blue, and light green. 2 oz. of red and dark blue, 1 oz. of yellow, gold, and dark brown.

NEEDLES: Size 3 and 5. One set of double-point needles, size 3.

GAUGE: 6 sts = 1 inch; 7½ rows = 1 inch, using size 5 needles.

SIZE: These directions are for a size 10 30-inch finished garment. Measurements are as follows: length to underarm 13 inches, length to shoulder 20 inches, length of sleeve to underarm 15½ inches.

To alter size see instructions for SIZING.

FRONT: With size 3 needles, cast on 80 sts. Work in K1, P1, ribbing for 3 inches. Change to size 5 needles and increase 8 sts evenly spaced on next row, working in st st. Continue in st st and work the charted design, binding off and decreasing as indicated. Place 14 sts in center of front on holder for neck.

BACK: Work back to match front using chart for pattern. Fill in pattern at neck with designs being used and place 26 sts in center of back on holder for neck.

SLEEVES: Cast on 40 sts on size 3 needles and work in ribbing K1, P1, for 3 inches. Change to size 5 needles and increase 8 sts evenly spaced in next row using st st. Work sleeves according to charted design.

Sew shoulder seams.

NECK: With size 3 double-point needles, K cross sts on back holder with right side facing. Pick up and K 56 sts to right shoulder (including sts on front holder). K1, P1, in ribbing on 80 sts for 1 inch. Bind off loosely in ribbing.

Sew sleeves in place. Sew underarm and sleeve seams. Weave in loose threads.

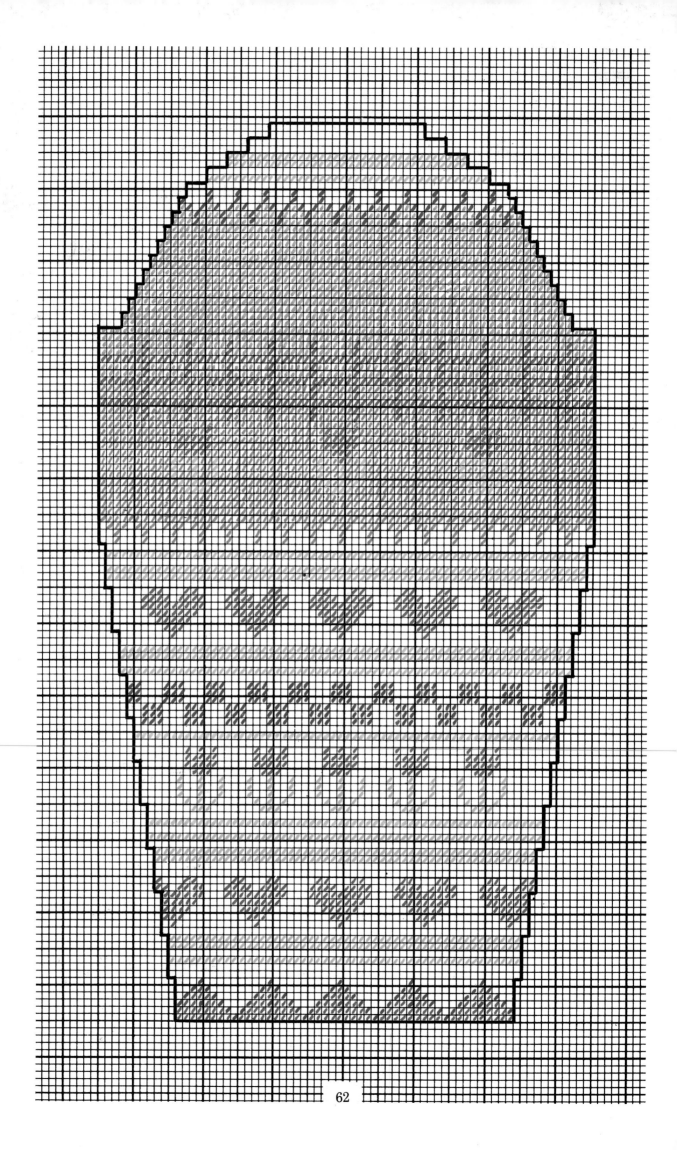

Country Goose Cardigan

COUNTRY GOOSE CARDIGAN

Use the basic instructions for the Country Goose Pullover and work the front as follows:

LEFT FRONT: With size 3 needles cast on 37 sts. Work in K1, P1, ribbing for 3 inches. Change to size 5 needles and increase 3 sts evenly spaced on next row using st st. Continue in st st working pattern according to charted design. Sts at center front of neck are placed on a holder for neck band.

RIGHT FRONT: Work as left front, but using chart for right front.

BACK: Work same as back for pullover.

BUTTON-HOLE BAND: Cast on 11 sts with size 3 needles. Work 4 rows K1, P1, ribbing. Next row: K1, P1, twice. Cast off 3 sts. K1, P1, twice. Next row: K1, P1, twice. Cast on 3 sts. K1, P1, twice. Work 18 rows in K1, P1, ribbing. Continue as above until 7 buttonholes in all have been worked. Rib 16 more rows. Place sts on holder.

Work band for other side omitting buttonholes.

Sew buttonhole band to right front and plain band to left front.
Sew shoulder seams.

NECKBAND: Work with right side facing. Rib across sts on buttonhole band using size 3 needles. Pick up and K sts on holder from right front neck, across sts from back holder, across sts from left front and left band (107 sts).
Rib one row.
2nd and 3rd rows: Buttonhole as before.
Work 4 more rows in K1, P1, ribbing.
Bind off in ribbing.

Sew sleeves in place. Sew underarm and sleeve seams. Weave in loose threads.

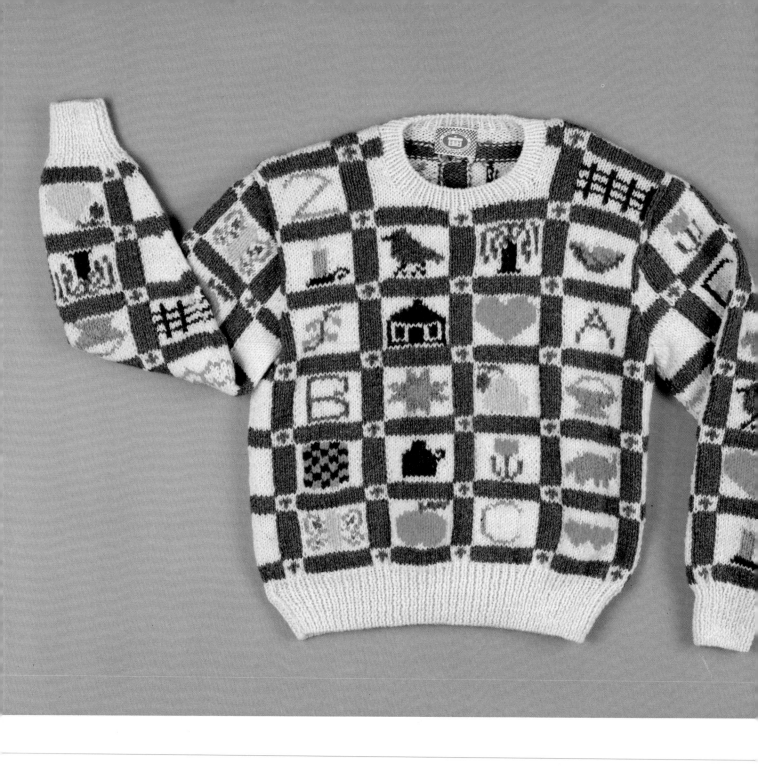

Patchwork Sampler
Crew-Neck Pullover

PATCHWORK SAMPLER CREW-NECK PULLOVER

We did this sweater for adults and it was tremendously popular. We had many, many requests for it in a child's size. Inspired by an old quilt, the inside motifs can be personalized to make it a very special sweater. Don't be afraid to use your imagination and create your own blocks. A super sweater and a great way to use up yarn leftovers.

MATERIALS: 10 to 12 oz. background color in featherweight knitting worsted, Shetland, sport-weight, or other yarn recommended for gauge below. 4 to 6 oz. color for solid bands. Various amounts of other colors for designs inside block. (These can be knit in or duplicate stitched later.)

NEEDLES: Size 3 and 5. One set of double-point needles, size 3.

GAUGE: 6 sts = 1 inch; 7½ rows = 1 inch, using size 5 needles.

SIZE: These directions are for a size 10 30-inch finished garment. Measurements are as follows: length to underarm 13 inches, length to shoulder 20 inches, length of sleeve to underarm 15½ inches.

To alter size see instructions for SIZING.

FRONT: With size 3 needles, cast on 80 sts. Work in K1, P1, ribbing for 3 inches. Change to size 5 needles and increase 8 sts evenly spaced on next row, working in st st. Continue in st st and work the charted design, binding off and decreasing as indicated. Place 14 sts in center of front on holder for neck.

BACK: Work back to match front using chart for pattern. Fill in pattern at neck with designs being used and place 26 sts in center of back on holder for neck.

SLEEVES: Cast on 40 sts on size 3 needles and work in ribbing K1, P1, for 3 inches. Change to size 5 needles and increase 8 sts evenly spaced in next row using st st. Work sleeves according to charted design.

Sew shoulder seams.

NECK: With size 3 double-point needles, K across sts on back holder with right side facing. Pick up and K 56 sts to right shoulder (including sts on front holder). K1, P1, in ribbing on 80 sts for 1 inch. Bind off loosely in ribbing.

Sew sleeves in place. Sew underarm and sleeve seams. Weave in loose threads.

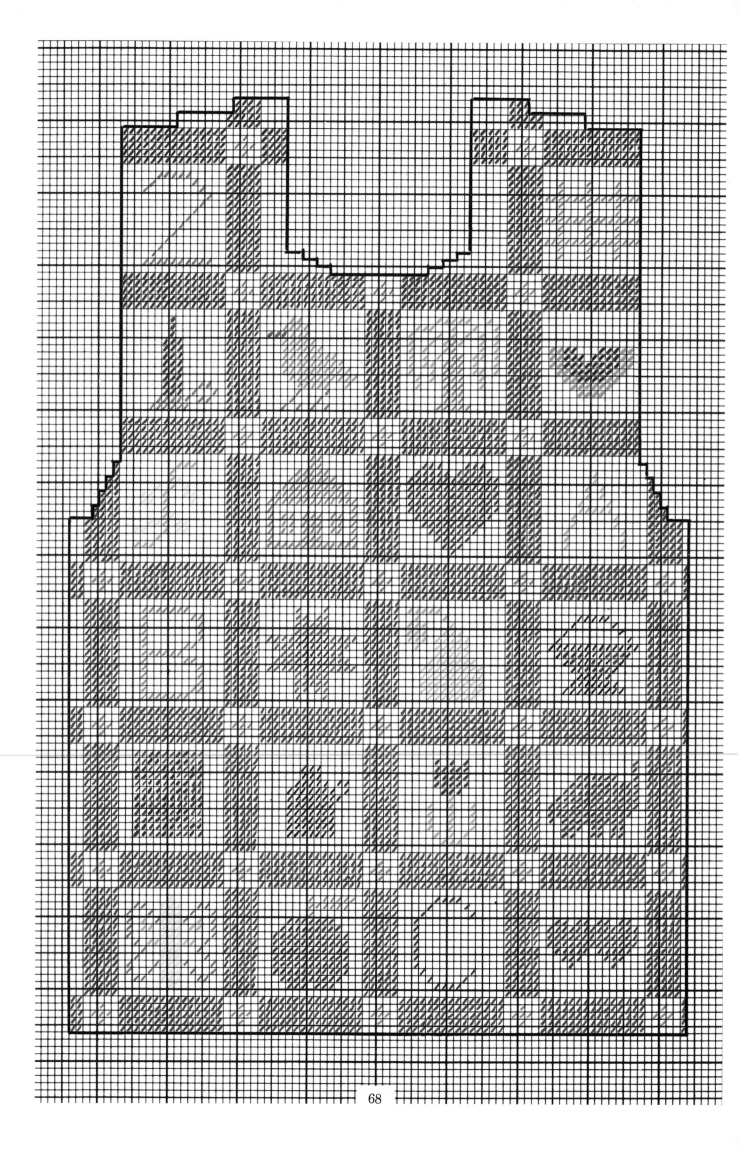

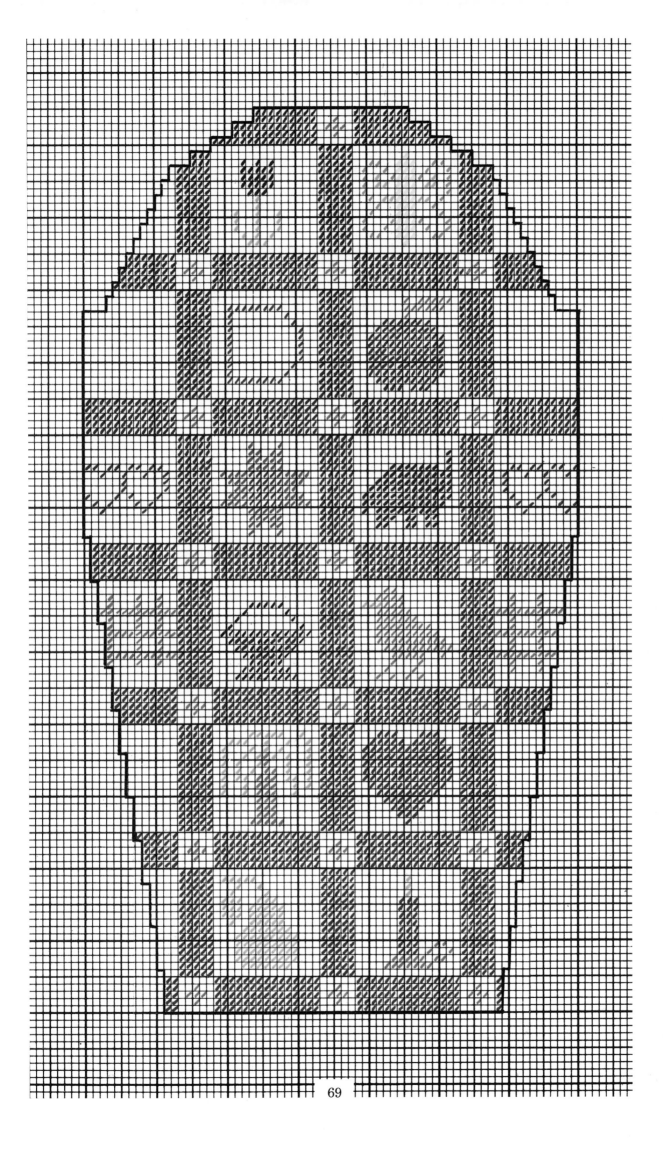

Schoolhouse Crew-Neck Pullover

SCHOOLHOUSE CREW-NECK PULLOVER

An appropriate pattern for the young set, the Schoolhouse is a real classic! Worked in a red, white, and blue traditional scheme, and adapted from a 19th-century quilt pattern, this motif has been effectively used on pottery, stationery, bags, and boxes. It's a great sweater and works up quickly.

MATERIALS: 12 to 16 oz. of featherweight knitting worsted, Shetland, sport-weight, or other yarn to give recommended gauge below, in main color. 3 to 4 oz. of two contrasting colors for pattern.

NEEDLES: Size 3 and 5. One set of double-point needles, size 3.

GAUGE: 6 sts = 1 inch; 7½ rows = 1 inch, using size 5 needles.

SIZE: These directions are for a size 10 30-inch finished garment. Measurements are as follows: length to underarm 13 inches, length to shoulder 20 inches, length of sleeve to underarm 15½ inches.

To alter size see instructions for SIZING.

FRONT: With size 3 needles, cast on 80 sts. Work in K1, P1, ribbing for 3 inches. Change to size 5 needles and increase 8 sts evenly spaced on next row, working in st st. Continue in st st and work the charted design, binding off and decreasing as indicated. Place 14 sts in center of front on holder for neck.

BACK: Work back to match front using chart for pattern. Fill in pattern at neck with designs being used and place 26 sts in center of back on holder for neck.

SLEEVES: Cast on 40 sts on size 3 needles and work in ribbing K1, P1, for 3 inches. Change to size 5 needles and increase 8 sts evenly spaced in next row using st st. Work sleeves according to charted design.

Sew shoulder seams.

NECK: With size 3 double-point needles, K across sts on back holder with right side facing. Pick up and K 56 sts to right shoulder (including sts on front holder). K1, P1, in ribbing on 80 sts for 1 inch. Bind off loosely in ribbing.

Sew sleeves in place. Sew underarm and sleeve seams. Weave in loose threads.

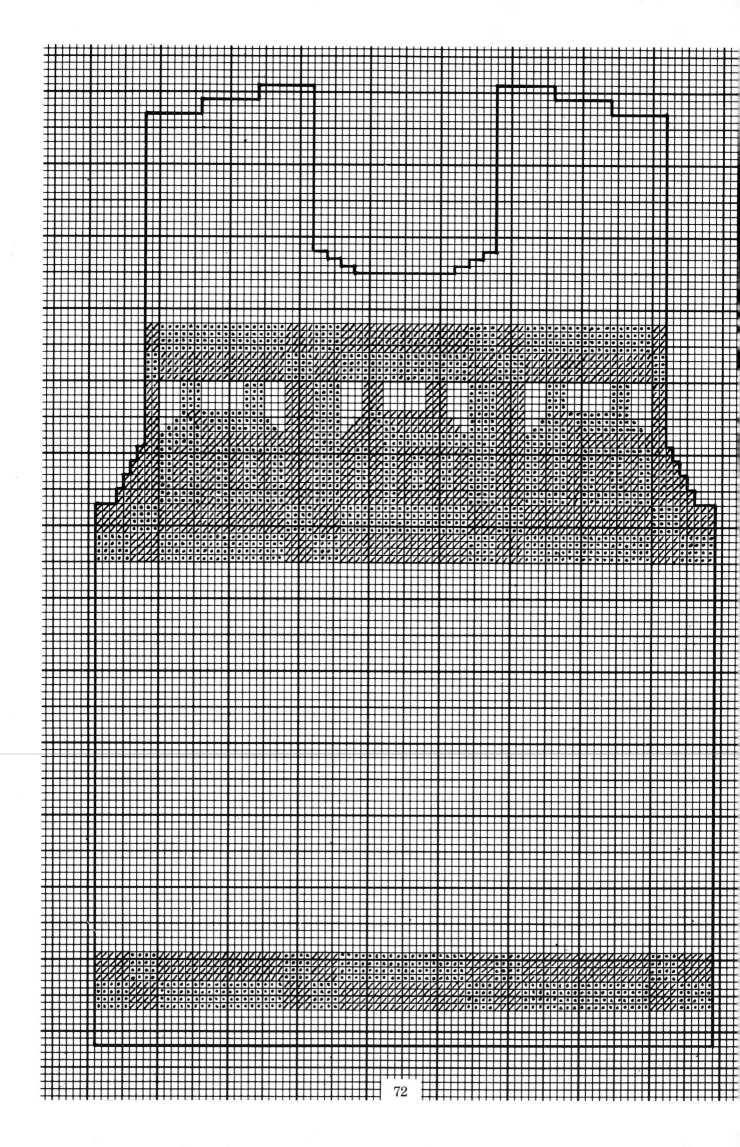

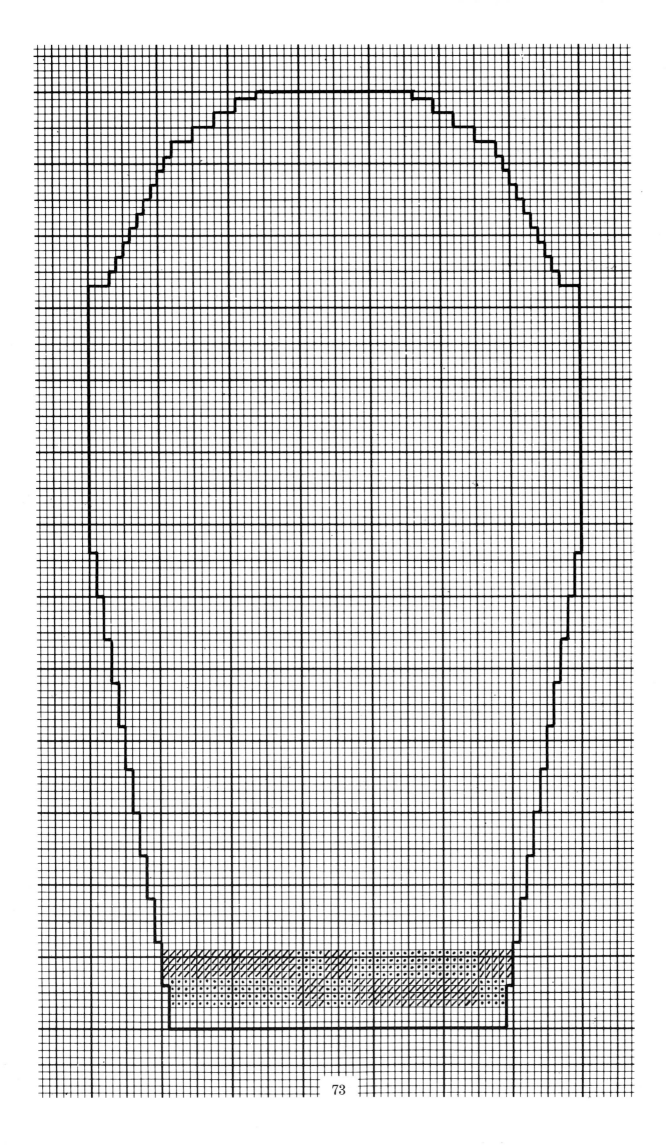

Diamonds Crew-Neck Pullover

DIAMONDS CREW-NECK PULLOVER

This easy geometric pattern is great for boys or girls. A stunning classic in contrasting colors, it is a wonderful alternative to the traditional argyle.

MATERIALS: 12 to 15 oz. background color in featherweight knitting worsted, Shetland, sport-weight, or other yarn recommended for gauge below. 2 to 3 oz. of contrasting color for diamonds.

NEEDLES: Size 3 and 5. One set of double-point needles, size 3.

GAUGE: 6 sts = 1 inch; 7½ rows = 1 inch, using size 5 needles.

SIZE: These directions are for a size 10 30-inch finished garment. Measurements are as follows: length to underarm 13 inches, length to shoulder 20 inches, length of sleeve to underarm 15½ inches.

To alter size see instructions for SIZING.

FRONT: With size 3 needles, cast on 80 sts. Work in K1, P1, ribbing for 3 inches. Change to size 5 needles and increase 8 sts evenly spaced on next row, working in st st. Continue in st st and work the charted design, binding off and decreasing as indicated. Place 14 sts in center of front on holder for neck.

BACK: Work back to match front using chart for pattern. Fill in pattern at neck with designs being used and place 26 sts in center of back on holder for neck.

SLEEVES: Cast on 40 sts on size 3 needles and work in ribbing K1, P1, for 3 inches. Change to size 5 needles and increase 8 sts evenly spaced in next row using st st. Work sleeves according to charted design.

Sew shoulder seams.

NECK: With size 3 double-point needles, K across sts on back holder with right side facing. Pick up and K 56 sts to right shoulder (including sts on front holder). K1, P1, in ribbing on 80 sts for 1 inch. Bind off loosely in ribbing.

Sew sleeves in place. Sew underarm and sleeve seams. Weave in loose threads.

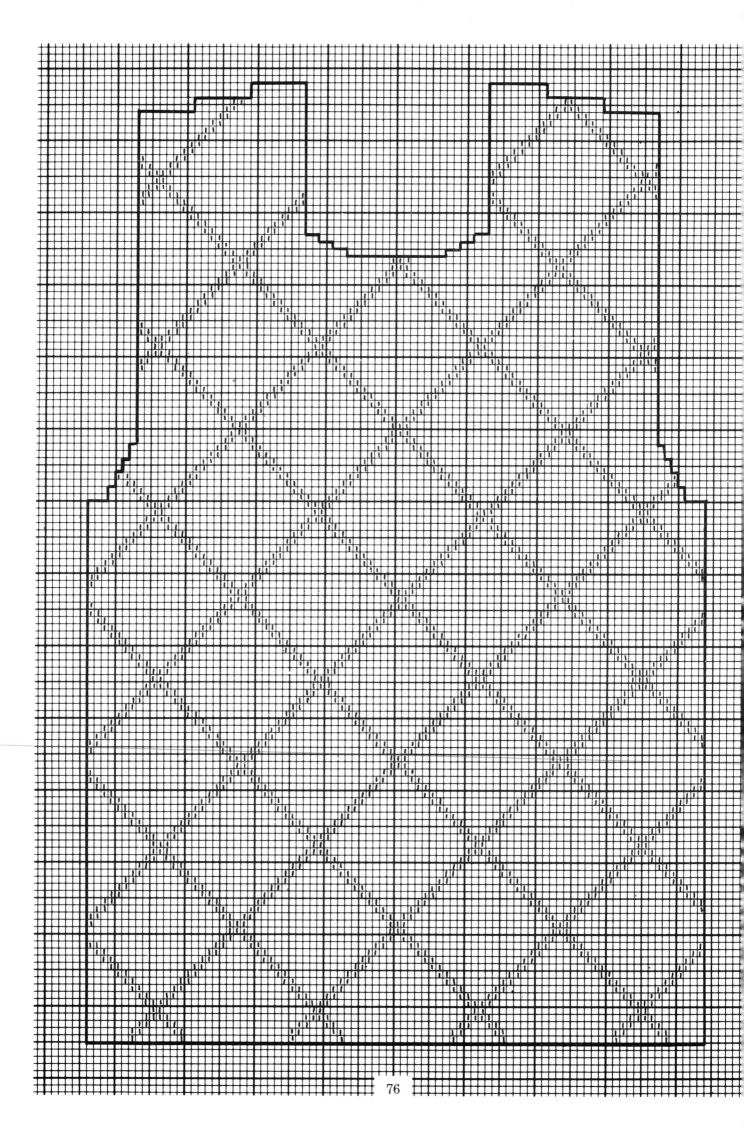

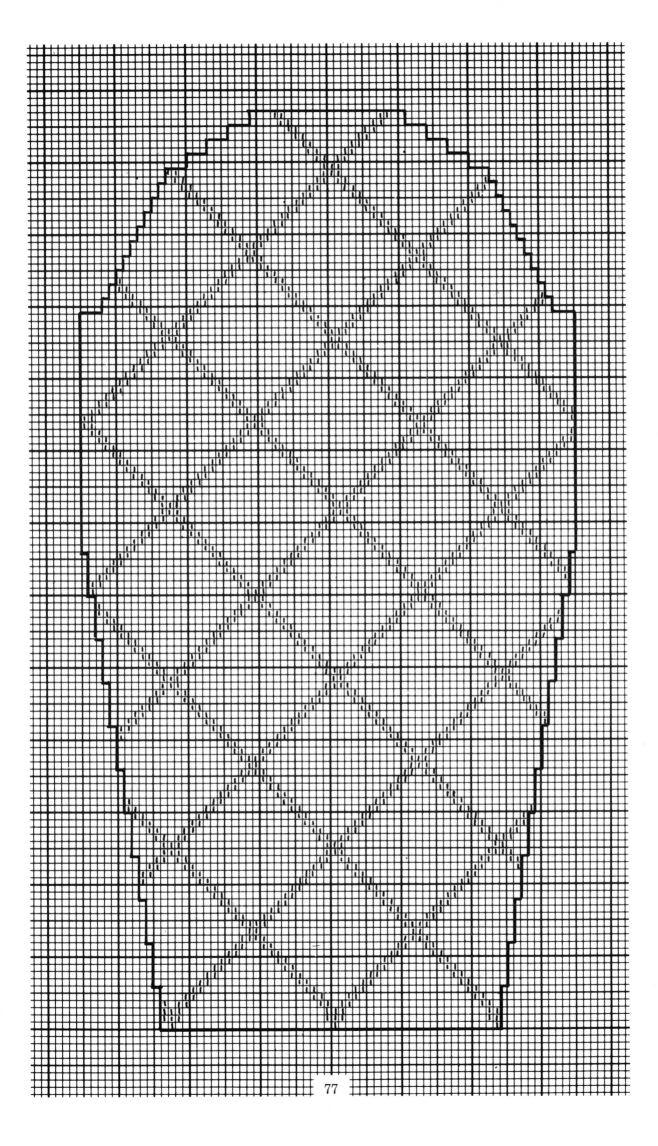

Sampler Crew-Neck Pullover

SAMPLER CREW-NECK PULLOVER

In this country's early beginnings sampler making was an important part of every girl's education. Day schools and boarding schools were prevalent and regional characteristics can be found on many of the samplers that have been handed down through generations. This design is an adaptation of a Balch School sampler wrought in Rhode Island in the late 18th century.

MATERIALS: 14 to 16 oz. off-white or other background color in feather-weight knitting worsted, Shetland, sport-weight, or other yarn recommended for gauge below. 1 oz. or less of each of dark brown, tan, yellow, dark green, red, blue, and light green.

NEEDLES: Size 3 and 5. One set of double-point needles, size 3.

GAUGE: 6 sts = 1 inch; 7½ rows = 1 inch, using size 5 needles.

SIZE: These directions are for a size 10 30-inch finished garment. Measurements are as follows: length to underarm 13 inches, length to shoulder 20 inches, length of sleeve to underarm 15½ inches.

To alter size see instructions for SIZING.

FRONT: With size 3 needles, cast on 80 sts. Work in K1, P1, ribbing for 3 inches. Change to size 5 needles and increase 8 sts evenly spaced on next row, working in st st. Continue in st st and work the charted design, binding off and decreasing as indicated. Place 14 sts in center of front on holder for neck.

BACK: Work back to match front using chart for pattern. Fill in pattern at neck with designs being used and place 26 sts in center of back on holder for neck.

SLEEVES: Cast on 40 sts on size 3 needles and work in ribbing K1, P1, for 3 inches. Change to size 5 needles and increase 8 sts evenly spaced in next row using st st. Work sleeves according to charted design.

Sew shoulder seams.

NECK: With size 3 double-point needles, K across sts on back holder with right side facing. Pick up and K 56 sts to right shoulder (including sts on front holder). K1, P1, in ribbing on 80 sts for 1 inch. Bind off loosely in ribbing.

Sew sleeves in place. Sew underarm and sleeve seams. Weave in loose threads.

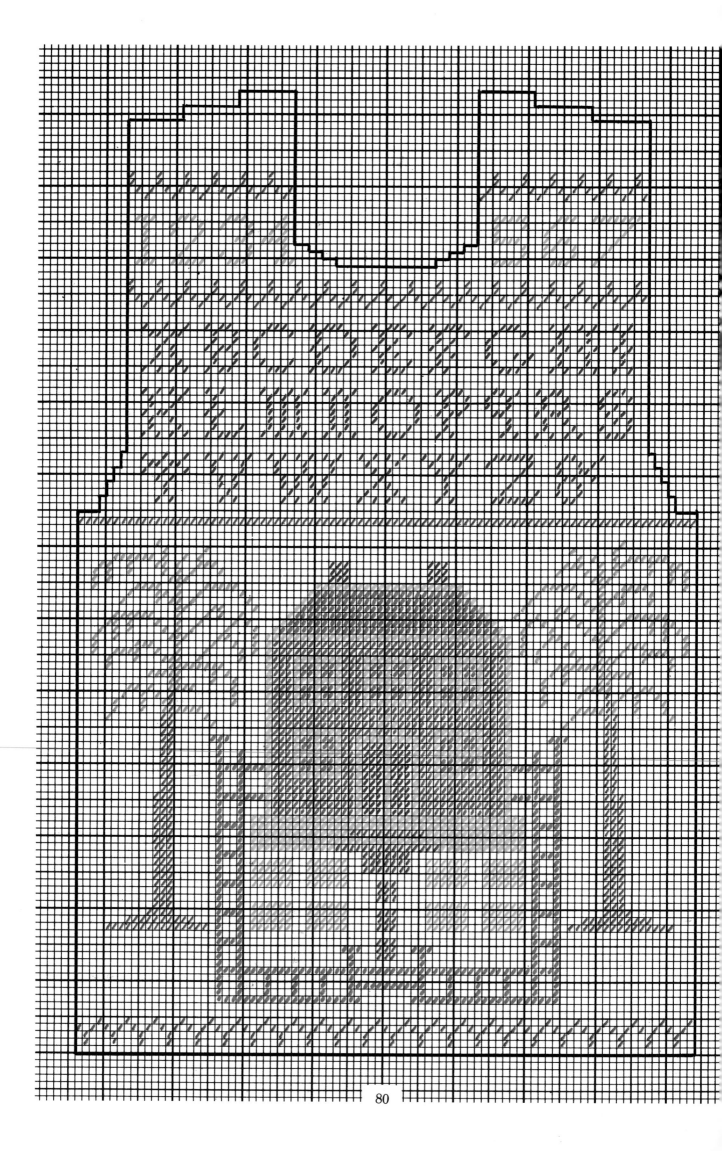

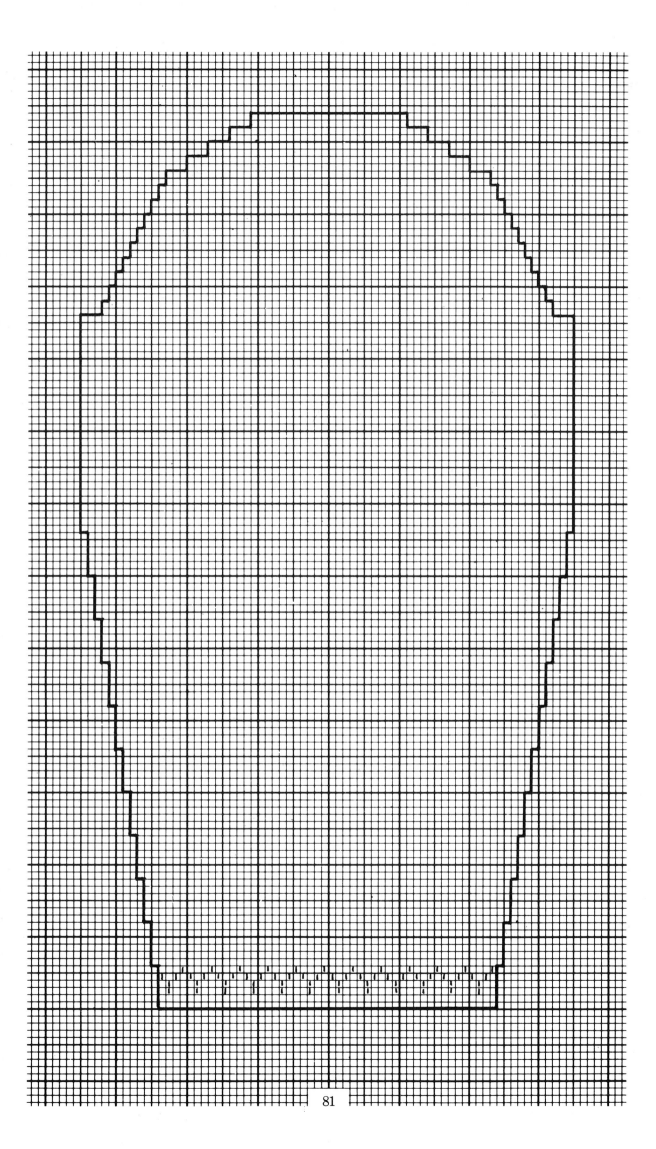

Irish Chain Crew-Neck Pullover

IRISH CHAIN CREW-NECK PULLOVER

Inspired by the popular 19th-century Irish Chain quilt pattern, this is a classic design and a super alternative to the standard plaids and checks. It is great in any color combination and is also interesting with texture variations between the small squares and the background color.

MATERIALS: 15 to 20 oz. main color and 4 to 6 oz. of contrasting color in featherweight knitting worsted, Shetland, sport-weight, or other yarn recommended for gauge below.

NEEDLES: Size 3 and 5. One set of double-point needles, size 3.

GAUGE: 6 sts = 1 inch; 7½ rows = 1 inch, using size 5 needles.

SIZE: These directions are for a size 10 30-inch finished garment. Measurements are as follows: length to underarm 13 inches, length to shoulder 20 inches, length of sleeve to underarm 15½ inches.

To alter size see instructions for SIZING.

FRONT: With size 3 needles, cast on 80 sts. Work in K1, P1, ribbing for 3 inches. Change to size 5 needles and increase 8 sts evenly spaced on next row, working in st st. Continue in st st and work the charted design, binding off and decreasing as indicated. Place 14 sts in center of front on holder for neck.

BACK: Work back to match front using chart for pattern. Fill in pattern at neck with designs being used and place 26 sts in center of back on holder for neck.

SLEEVES: Cast on 40 sts on size 3 needles and work in ribbing K1, P1, for 3 inches. Change to size 5 needles and increase 8 sts evenly spaced in next row using st st. Work sleeves according to charted design.

Sew shoulder seams.

NECK: With size 3 double-point needles, K across sts on back holder with right side facing. Pick up and K 56 sts to right shoulder (including sts on front holder). K1, P1, in ribbing on 80 sts for 1 inch. Bind off loosely in ribbing.

Sew sleeves in place. Sew underarm and sleeve seams. Weave in loose threads.

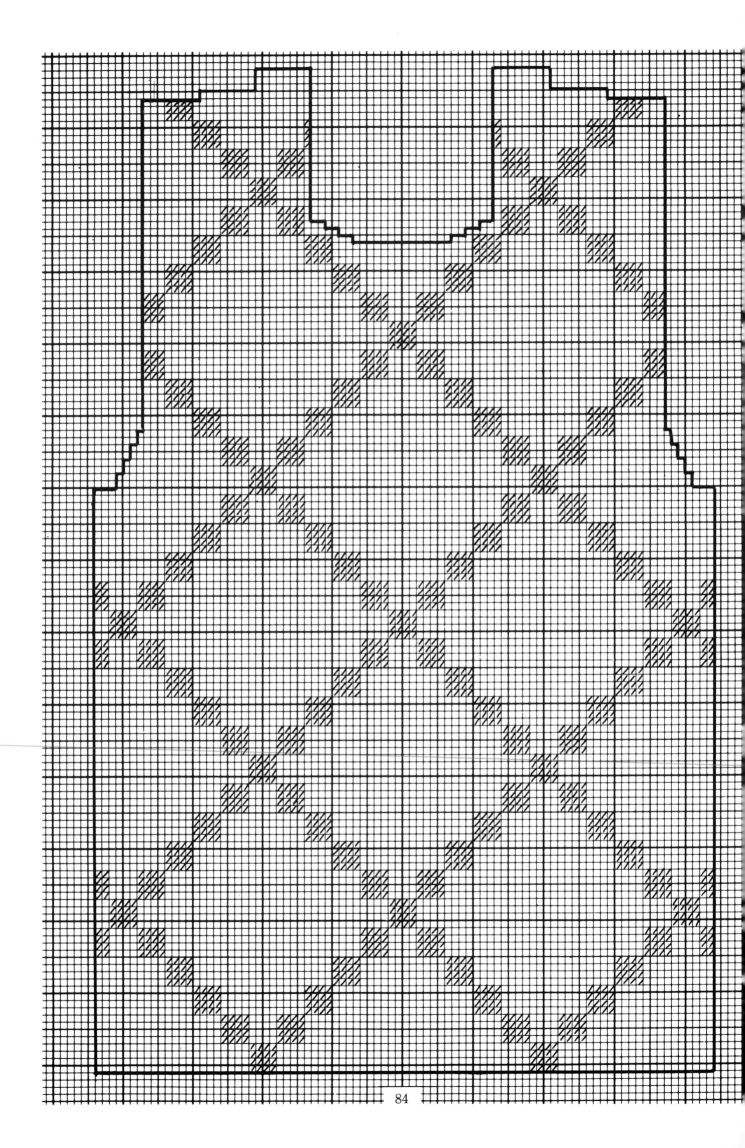

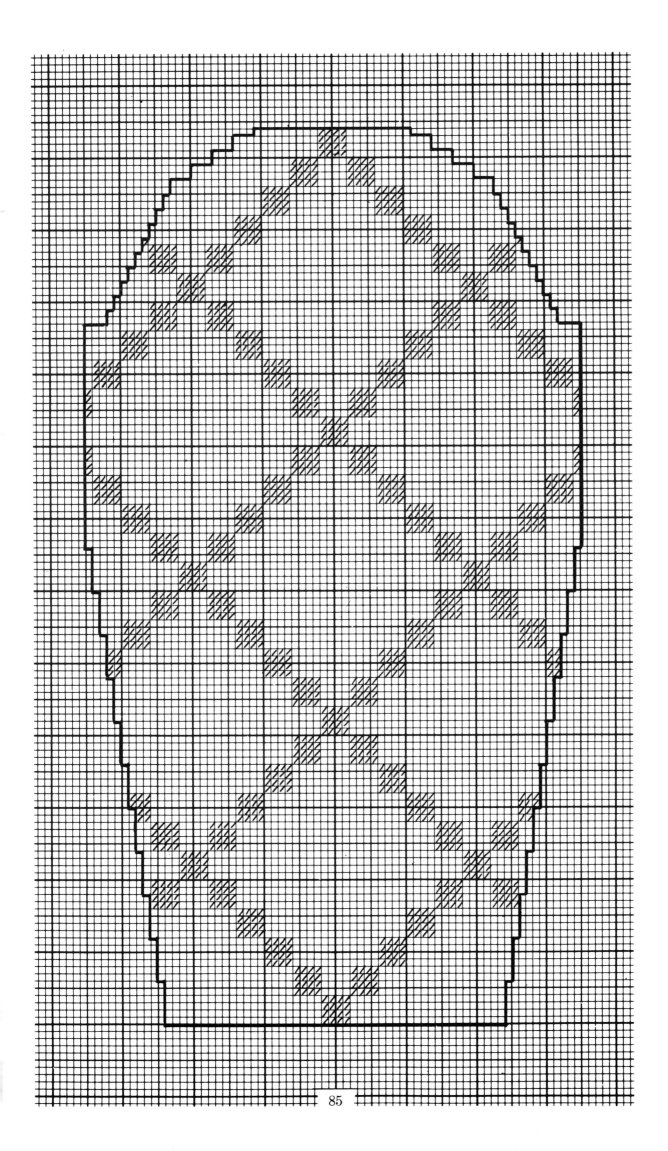

Flying Geese Crew-Neck Pullover

FLYING GEESE CREW-NECK PULLOVER

A favorite old quilt design, this has adapted beautifully to a sweater pattern. The quilts were often made from scraps of old fabric, thus the random colors. This also works up well by knitting all of the triangles in one color, the background in a second, and the stripes and ribbing in a third. Use your imagination!

MATERIALS: 7 oz. featherweight knitting worsted, Shetland, sport-weight, or other yarn recommended for gauge below, for triangles. 7 oz. contrasting color for ribbing and stripes. 7 oz. of off-white or other color for background.

NEEDLES: Size 3 and 5. One set of double-point needles, size 3.

GAUGE: 6 sts = 1 inch; 7½ rows = 1 inch, using size 5 needles.

SIZE: These directions are for a size 10 30-inch finished garment. Measurements are as follows: length to underarm 13 inches, length to shoulder 20 inches, length of sleeve to underarm 15½ inches.

To alter size see instructions for SIZING.

FRONT: With size 3 needles, cast on 80 sts. Work in K1, P1, ribbing for 3 inches. Change to size 5 needles and increase 8 sts evenly spaced on next row, working in st st. Continue in st st and work the charted design, binding off and decreasing as indicated. Place 14 sts in center of front on holder for neck.

BACK: Work back to match front using chart for pattern. Fill in pattern at neck with designs being used and place 26 sts in center of back on holder for neck.

SLEEVES: Cast on 40 sts on size 3 needles and work in ribbing K1, P1, for 3 inches. Change to size 5 needles and increase 8 sts evenly spaced in next row using st st. Work sleeves according to charted design.

Sew shoulder seams.

NECK: With size 3 double-point needles, K across sts on back holder with right side facing. Pick up and K 56 sts to right shoulder (including sts on front holder). K1, P1, in ribbing on 80 sts for 1 inch. Bind off loosely in ribbing.

Sew sleeves in place. Sew underarm and sleeve seams. Weave in loose threads.

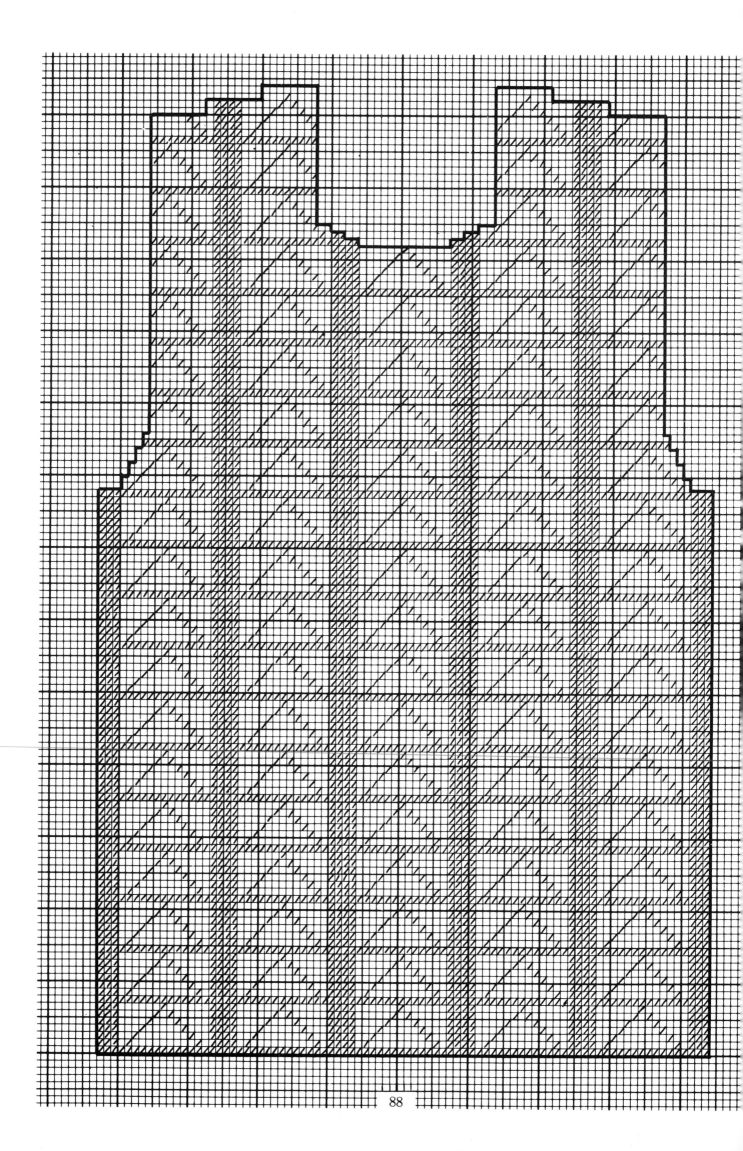

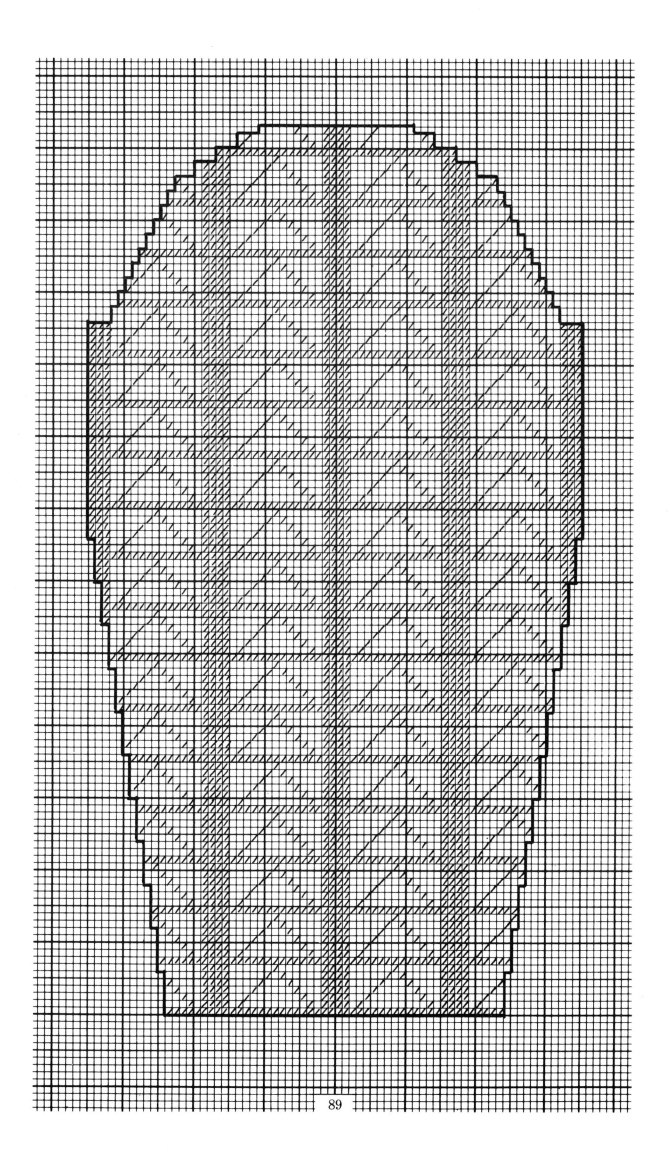

Flamingo and Palm Tree
Collared Pullover

FLAMINGO AND PALM TREE COLLARED PULLOVER

An Art Deco rendition of Country, this is a popular motif with girls 10 to 14. It's "in," lots of fun, and quick to knit. It works up to a BIG oversize sweater—one they'll wear for a long, long time.

MATERIALS: 14 to 16 oz. cotton or wool in weight recommended for gauge below, in background color. 2 to 3 oz. each of brown, sand, blue, bright green, light brown, and hot pink.

NEEDLES: Size 3 and 5. Size 3 circular needle.

GAUGE: 6 sts = 1 inch; 6½–8 rows = 1 inch. Check yarn band as cottons are very irregular. Calculate finished length and add or delete rows if necessary.

SIZE: These directions are for a size 10 to 14 oversize sweater. Measure arm and underarm to length desired and add or delete rows as needed. Finished chest measurement is 33½ inches.

FRONT: With smaller needles and main color, cast on 94 sts. Work in K2, P2, ribbing for 1½ inches increasing 6 sts across last row. Change to larger needles and follow graph, increasing, decreasing, and binding off as indicated.

BACK: Work as for front, omitting tree and flamingo and continuing stripes across bottom, matching sides. Increase, decrease and bind off as shown. Place center sts on holder for neck.

SLEEVES: With smaller needles, cast on 40 sts in main color. Work in K2, P2, ribbing for 1½ inches, increasing 10 sts evenly spaced across last row. Work in st st following charted design, increasing, decreasing, and binding off as indicated.

Sew shoulder seams.

COLLAR: With right side facing, and circular needle, begin at center front, pick up and K21 sts along right front neck to shoulder, 34 sts along back neck and 21 sts along left neck to center front, 76 sts. Join and place marker for beginning of round. NEXT ROUND: K1, *P2, K2; rep from *, end K1. Repeat last round 3 more times. Continue working back and forth in rib as follows: NEXT ROUND (right side): decrease 1 st, rib to last st, decrease 1 st. Continue in K2, P2, until collar measures 3 inches. Bind off in ribbing.

FINISHING: Sew top of sleeves to shoulders. Sew side and sleeve seams. Weave in threads.

KEY: ✗ BLUE, ∤ GREEN, ✦ PALE PINK,
╱ PINK, · BROWN, − TAN

Windowpane Crew-Neck Pullover

WINDOWPANE CREW-NECK PULLOVER

A simple, classic design used by the Shakers for woven twill blankets, this makes up into a wonderful traditional sweater. Nice for either sex and can be worn for dress or casual. The vertical lines can be worked in duplicate stitch, chain stitch, or knitted in.

MATERIALS: 15 to 20 oz. main color in featherweight knitting worsted, Shetland, sport-weight, or other yarn recommended for gauge below. 2 to 4 oz. of a contrasting color.

NEEDLES: Size 3 and 5. One set of double-point needles, size 3.

GAUGE: 6 sts = 1 inch; 7½ rows = 1 inch, using size 5 needles.

SIZE: These directions are for a size 10 30-inch finished garment. Measurements are as follows: length to underarm 13 inches, length to shoulder 20 inches, length of sleeve to underarm 15½ inches.

To alter size see instructions for SIZING.

FRONT: With size 3 needles, cast on 80 sts. Work in K1, P1, ribbing for 3 inches. Change to size 5 needles and increase 8 sts evenly spaced on next row, working in st st. Continue in st st and work the charted design, binding off and decreasing as indicated. Place 14 sts in center of front on holder for neck.

BACK: Work back to match front using chart for pattern. Fill in pattern at neck with designs being used and place 26 sts in center of back on holder for neck.

SLEEVES: Cast on 40 sts on size 3 needles and work in ribbing K1, P1, for 3 inches. Change to size 5 needles and increase 8 sts evenly spaced in next row using st st. Work sleeves according to charted design.

Sew shoulder seams.

NECK: With size 3 double-point needles, K across sts on back holder with right side facing. Pick up and K 56 sts to right shoulder (including sts on front holder). K1, P1, in ribbing on 80 sts for 1 inch. Bind off loosely in ribbing.

Sew sleeves in place. Sew underarm and sleeve seams. Weave in loose threads.

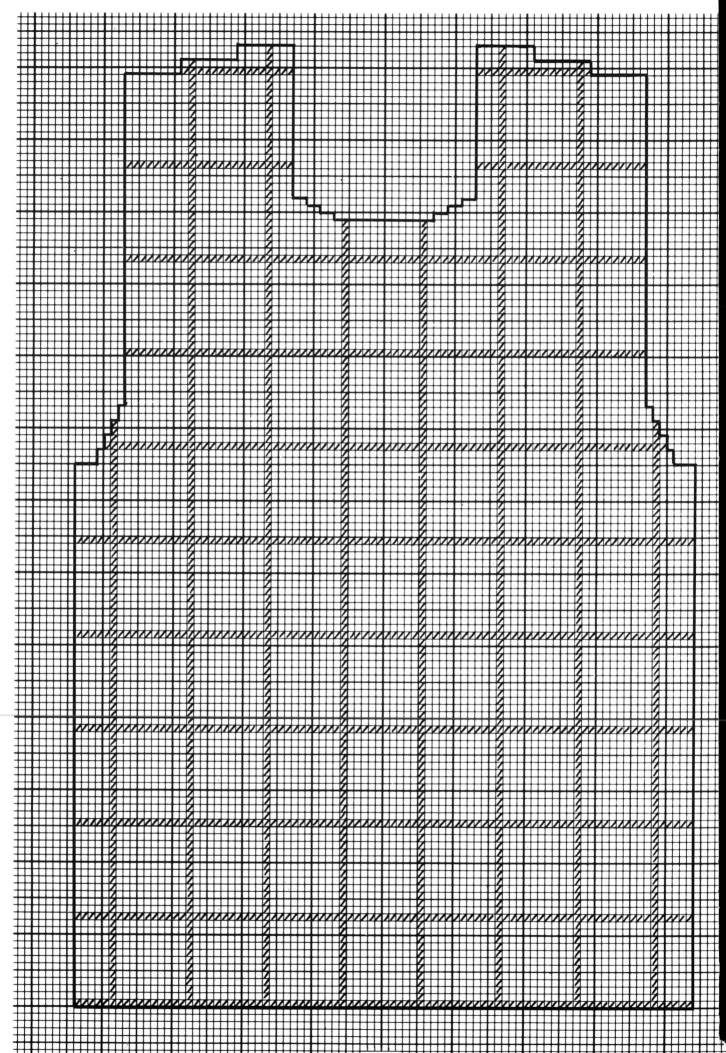

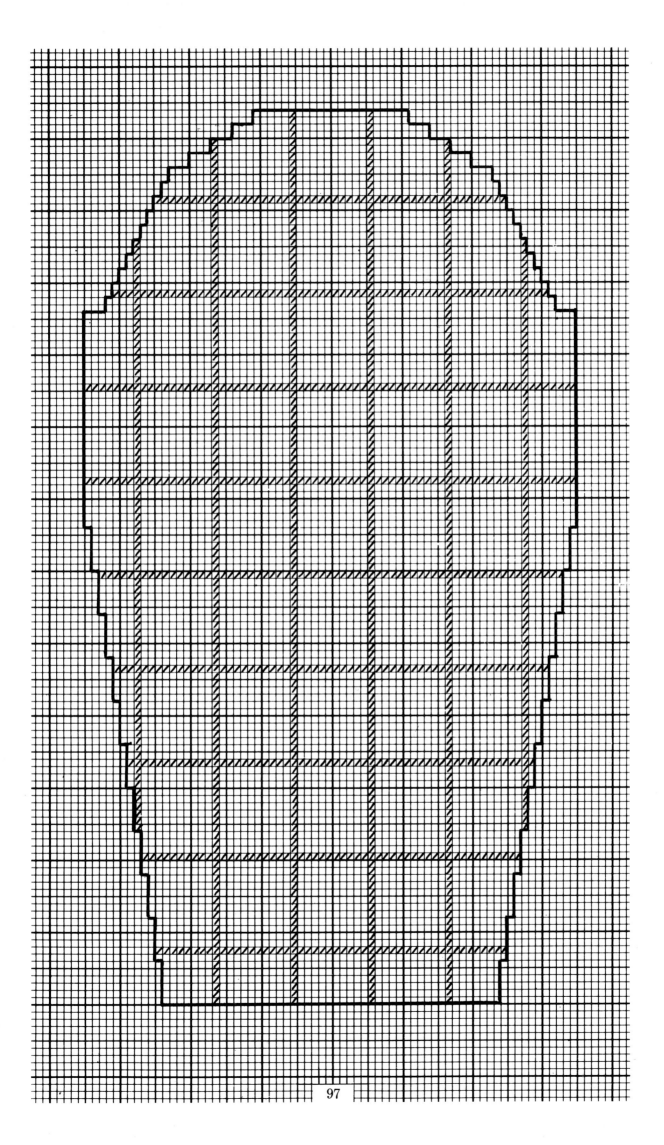

Double Irish Chain
Crew-Neck Pullover

DOUBLE IRISH CHAIN CREW-NECK PULLOVER

Boys and girls alike love this geometric-design sweater taken from a bold mid-19th-century quilt pattern. It's great both in monotone schemes and bright contrasting ones. Red, white, and blue are always a favorite, or the more classic colors we show here.

MATERIALS: 10 to 12 oz. of main color in featherweight knitting worsted, Shetland, sport-weight, or other yarn recommended for gauge below. 6 oz. of contrasting color for center squares. 8 to 10 oz. of a contrasting color for outside square.

NEEDLES: Size 3 and 5. One set of double-point needles, size 3.

GAUGE: 6 sts = 1 inch; 7½ rows = 1 inch, using size 5 needles.

SIZE: These directions are for a size 10 30-inch finished garment. Measurements are as follows: length to underarm 13 inches, length to shoulder 20 inches, length of sleeve to underarm 15½ inches.

To alter size see instructions for SIZING.

FRONT: With size 3 needles, cast on 80 sts. Work in K1, P1, ribbing for 3 inches. Change to size 5 needles and increase 8 sts evenly spaced on next row, working in st st. Continue in st st and work the charted design, binding off and decreasing as indicated. Place 14 sts in center of front on holder for neck.

BACK: Work back to match front using chart for pattern. Fill in pattern at neck with designs being used and place 26 sts in center of back on holder for neck.

SLEEVES: Cast on 40 sts on size 3 needles and work in ribbing K1, P1, for 3 inches. Change to size 5 needles and increase 8 sts evenly spaced in next row using st st. Work sleeves according to charted design.

Sew shoulder seams.

NECK: With size 3 double-point needles, K across sts on back holder with right side facing. Pick up and K 56 sts to right shoulder (including sts on front holder). K1, P1, in ribbing on 80 sts for 1 inch. Bind off loosely in ribbing.

Sew sleeves in place. Sew underarm and sleeve seams. Weave in loose threads.

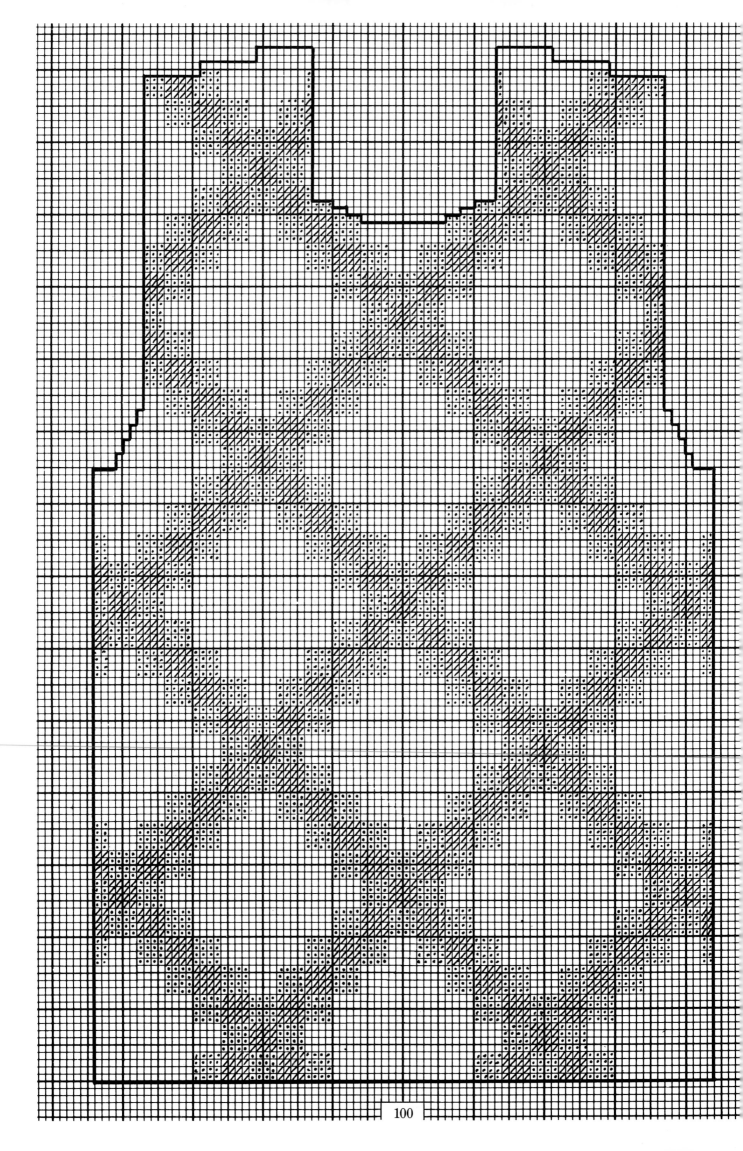

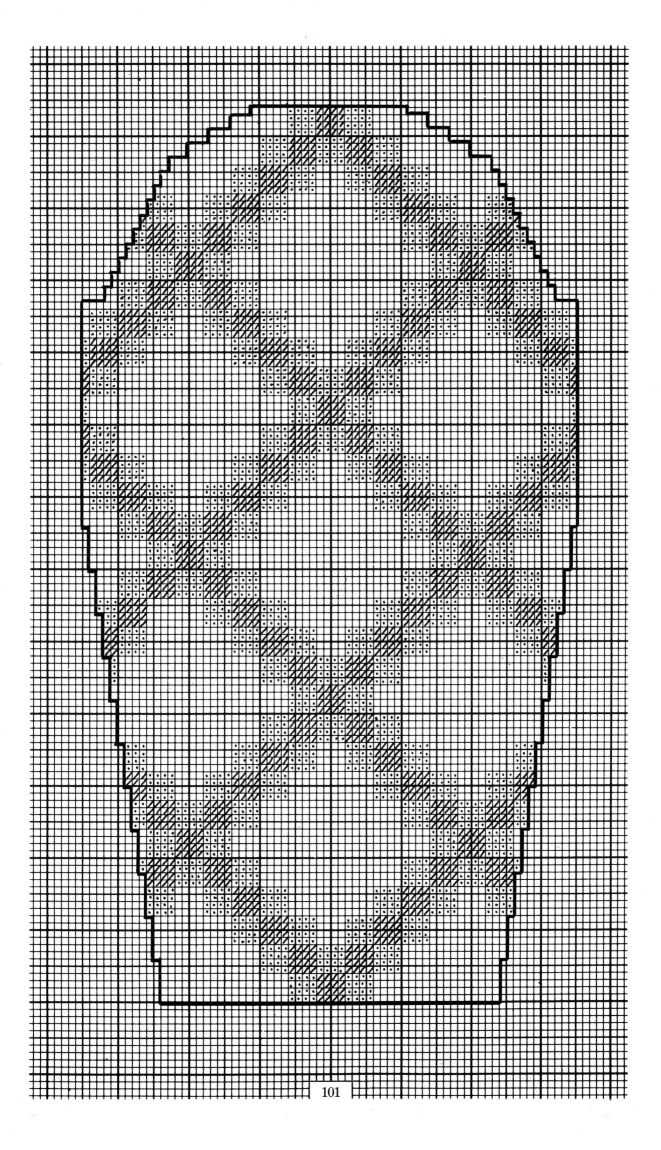

Moored Boats Crew-Neck Pullover

MOORED BOATS CREW-NECK PULLOVER

The "yachty" look of this sweater will make it a hit with boys and girls alike. Knit in two colors, the boats are silhouetted against the background. For lots of bright color, work the boats in different shades and make the sleeves multicolor stripes.

MATERIALS: 18 to 20 oz. of background color in featherweight worsted, Shetland, sport-weight, tweeds, or other yarn recommended for gauge below. 6 to 8 oz. of contrasting color or combination of colors for boats and stripes.

NEEDLES: Size 3 and 5. One set of double-point needles, size 3.

GAUGE: 6 sts = 1 inch; 7½ rows = 1 inch.

SIZE: These directions are for a size 12 with a finished chest measurement of 33 inches.

To alter size see instructions for SIZING.

NOTE: This is a drop shoulder and does not hit at the usual shoulder seam. Check sleeves for length while knitting.

FRONT: With main color and size 3 needles, cast on 84 sts and work in K1, P1, ribbing for 2 inches. Increase 16 sts evenly spaced across next row of ribbing. Change to larger needles and working in st st follow graphed design. Increase, decrease, and bind off as indicated. Place center sts of neck on holder for neck ribbing.

BACK: Work as for front, omitting central motif, but continuing stripes.

SLEEVES: With smaller needles and main color cast on 34 sts. Work in K1, P1, ribbing for 2 inches. Increase 10 sts in next row of ribbing, 44 sts. Change to larger needles and work in st st following charted design. Increase and bind off as indicated.

Sew shoulder seams.

NECK: With right sides facing and double-point needles, begin at right shoulder, pick up and K 32 sts along back neck, 44 sts along front neck, 76 sts. Work in K1, P1, ribbing for 1 inch. Bind off loosely in ribbing.

Sew sleeves to front and back. Sew sleeve and side seams.

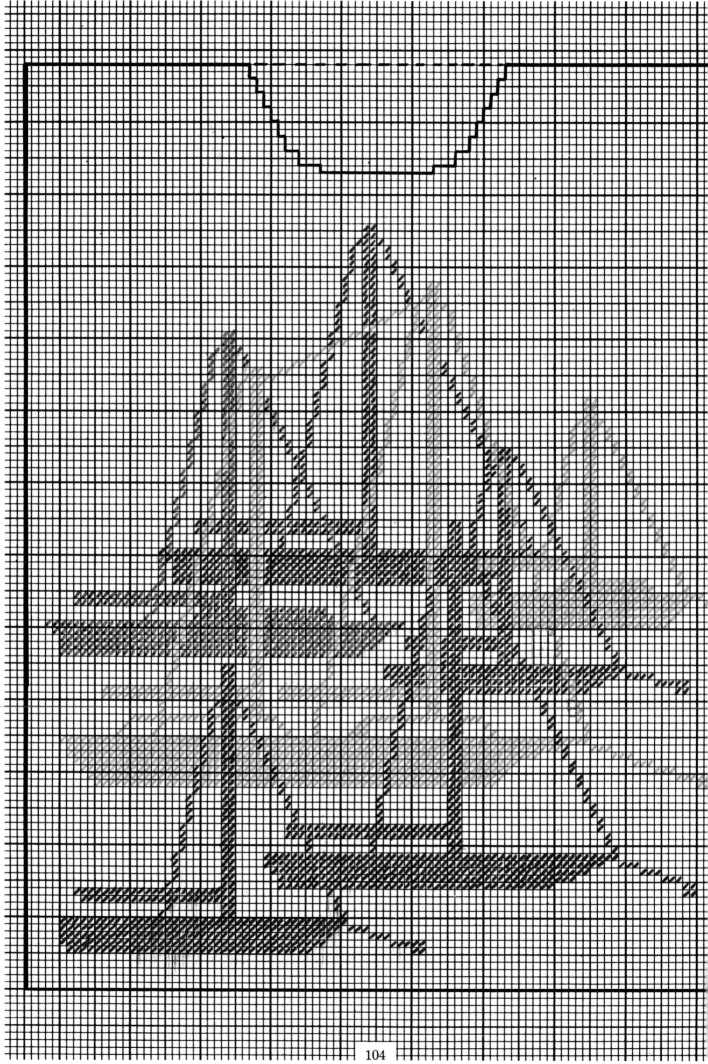

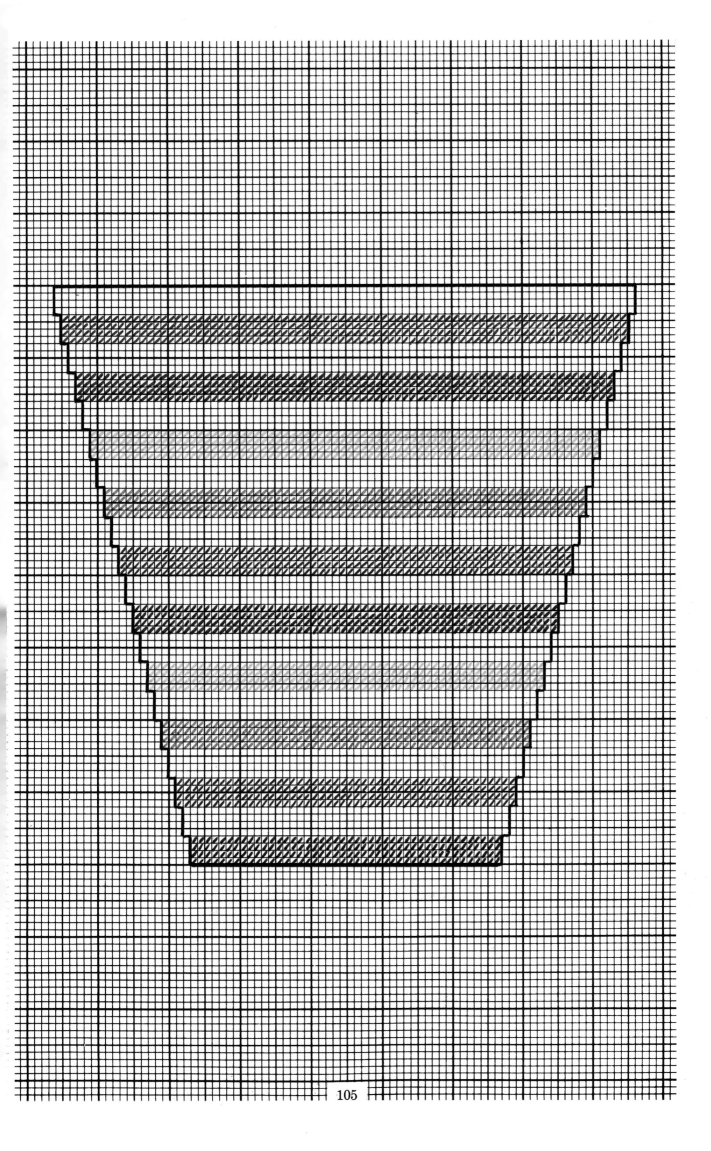

Christmas Goose Crew-Neck Pullover

CHRISTMAS GOOSE CREW-NECK PULLOVER

A special country, seasonal sweater, the traditional goose is decked out for the holidays with a big bow. Stripes give a candy cane look to the background and make for a festive Christmas sweater. It also looks great with a green background and white stripe.

MATERIALS: 12 to 15 oz. main color in featherweight knitting worsted, Shetland, sport-weight, or other yarn recommended for gauge below. 4 to 6 oz. of stripe color, 1 oz. of color for checkerboard frame, 1 oz. of color for goose, 1 oz. of background color inside frame. Small amount of color for ribbon, beak, feet, and eye.

NEEDLES: Size 3 and 5. One set of double-point needles, size 3.

GAUGE: 6 sts = 1 inch; 7½ rows = 1 inch.

SIZE: These directions are for a size 12 with a finished chest measurement of 33 inches.

To alter size see instructions for SIZING.

NOTE: This is a drop shoulder and does not hit at the usual shoulder seam. Check sleeves for length while knitting.

FRONT: With main color and size 3 needles, cast on 84 sts and work in K1, P1, ribbing for 2 inches. Increase 16 sts evenly spaced across next row of ribbing. Change to larger needles and working in st st follow graphed design. Increase, decrease, and bind off as indicated. Place center sts of neck on holder for neck ribbing.

BACK: Work as for front, omitting central motif, but continuing stripes.

SLEEVES: With smaller needles and main color cast on 34 sts. Work in K1, P1, ribbing for 2 inches. Increase 10 sts in next row of ribbing, 44 sts. Change to larger needles and work in st st following charted design. Increase and bind off as indicated.

Sew shoulder seams.

NECK: With right sides facing and double-point needles, begin at right shoulder, pick up and K 32 sts along back neck, 44 sts along front neck, 76 sts. Work in K1, P1, ribbing for 1 inch. Bind off loosely in ribbing.

Sew sleeves to front and back. Sew sleeve and side seams.

KEY: · DARK GREEN, ╱ TAN, ✚ RED, ✖ RED,
INSIDE FRAME-YELLOW

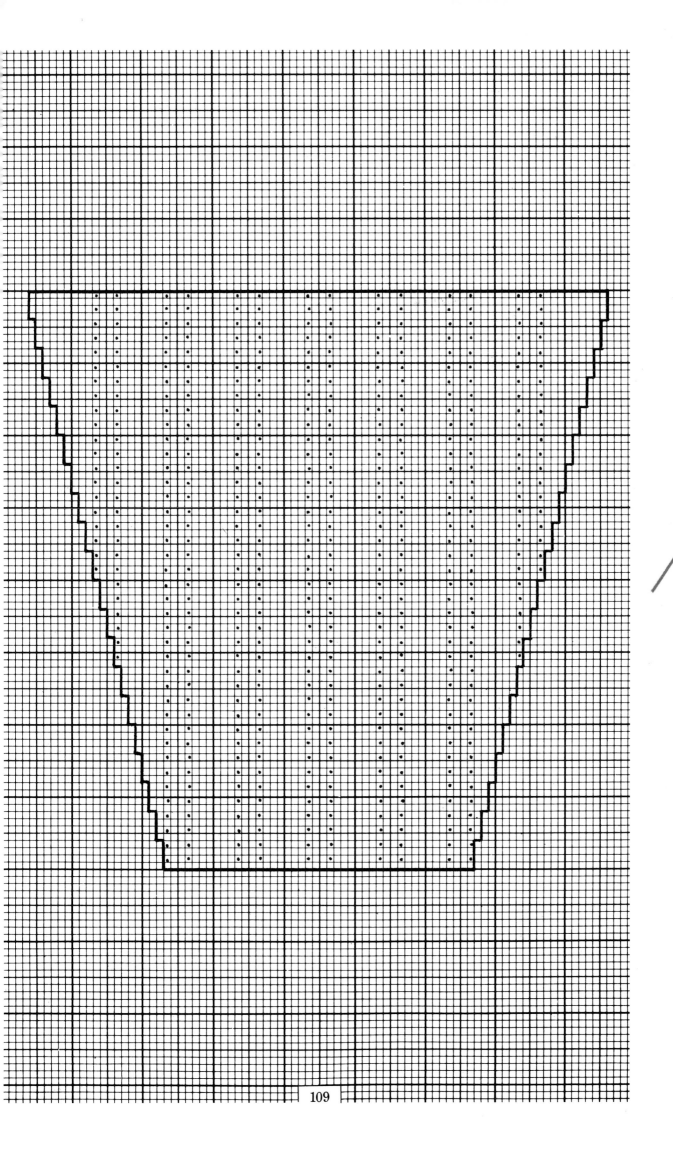

YARN MANUFACTURERS IN THE U.S.

If you have trouble finding the yarns you would like to use, contact these manufacturers for a list of the dealers nearest you.

ANDEAN YARNS
54 Industrial Way
Wilmington, Mass. 01887
(617) 657-7680
$3.00/color cards

ARMEN CORP.
(Chat Botte)
1400 Brevard Rd.
Asheville, N.C. 28806
(704) 667-9902

ARMOUR HANDCRAFTS INC.
(Bucilla)
150 Meadowland Pkwy.
Secaucus, N.J. 07094
(201) 330-9100

BERNAT YARN & CRAFT CORP.
Depot & Mendon Sts.
Uxbridge, Mass. 01569
(617) 278-2414

BOUQUET YARNS USA
51 Covert Ave.
Floral Park, N.Y. 11001
(516) 354-8537

BRUNSWICK WORSTED MILLS INC.
Brunswick Ave.
Moosup, Conn. 06354
(203) 564-2761

BUCILLA
(3 Suisses)
230 Fifth Ave.
New York, N.Y. 10021

CANDIDE YARNS
Woodbury, Conn. 06796

CASWELL SHEEP & WOOL CO.
Rt. 1, Box 135
Blanch, N.C. 27212
(919) 694-4838

CIRCULO YARNS INC.
(cotton)
7963 N.W. 14th St.
Miami, Fla. 33126
(305) 594-0404

COLUMBIA-MINERVA
230 Fifth Ave.
New York, N.Y. 10001
(212) 685-2907

CONSHOHOCKEN COTTON CO.
Ford Bridge Rd.
Conshohocken, Pa. 19428
(215) 825-4270

CRYSTAL PALACE YARNS
3006 San Pablo Ave.
Berkeley, Calif. 94702
(415) 548-9988

DYED IN THE WOOL, LTD.
252 W. 37th St.
New York, N.Y. 10018
(212) 563-6669

E'LITE SPECIALTY YARNS INC.
750 Suffolk St.
Lowell, Mass. 01854
(617) 453-2837

ERDOL YARNS LTD.
(designer yarns)
303 5th Ave.
Room 1109
New York, N.Y. 10016
(212) 725-0162
$5/color card

FAIR DINKUM IMPORTS
7525 Harold Ave.
Golden Valley, Minn. 55427
(612) 545-6471

FANTACIA, INC.
(distributor for Lana Gatto)
415 E. Beach Ave.
Inglewood, Calif. 90302
(213) 673-7914

JOSEPH GALLER
27 West 20th St.
New York, N.Y. 10011

GRANDOR INDUSTRIES, LTD.
(Sunbeam)
4031 Knobhill Drive
Sherman Oaks, Calif. 91403

HERRSCHNERS
999 Plaza Drive
Suite 660
Schaumburg, Ill. 60195
(312) 843-6931

S. & C. HUBER, AMERICAN CLASSICS
82 Plants Dam Road
East Lyme, Conn. 06333
(203) 739-0772
$3/color card

KENDEX CORP.
(Sirdar)
31332 Via Colinas #107
Westlake Village, Calif. 91362

KIWI IMPORTS, INC.
(Perendale)
54 Industrial Way
Wilmington, Mass. 01887
(617) 657-8566
(617) 938-0077

LAINES ANNY BLATT
24770 Crestview Ct.
Farmington Hills, Mich. 48018
(313) 474-2942

LION BRAND YARN CO.
1270 Broadway
New York, N.Y. 10001
(212) 736-7937

MERINO WOOL INC.
(Emu and Picaud)
230 Fifth Ave.
20th Floor
New York, N.Y. 10001

NOMOTTA YARNS, INC.
60 E. 42nd St. #3421
New York, N.Y. 10165
(212) 687-3361
(516) 933-0994

PHILDAR
6438 Dawson Boulevard
85 North
Norcross, Ga. 30093

PHILIPS IMPORTS
(Sunbeam)
P.O. Box 146
Port St. Joe, Fla. 32456

PINGOUIN-PROMAFIL CORP.
P.O. Box 100
Highway 45
Jamestown, S.C. 29453

REYNOLDS YARN INC.
15 Oser Ave.
Hauppauge, N.Y. 11788
(516) 582-9330

SCHAFFHAUSER
938 NW Couch
Portland, Ore. 97209
(503) 222-3022

SCHEEPJESWOL USA INC.
155 Lafayette Ave.
North White Plains, N.Y.
(800) 431-4040; in N.Y. (91

SHEPHERD WOOLS INC.
917 Industry Dr.
Seattle, Wash. 98188
(206) 575-0131

SUGAR RIVER YARNS
P.O. Box 663
New Glarus, Wis. 53574

TAHKI IMPORTS LTD.
92 Kennedy St.
Hackensack, N.J. 07601
(201) 489-9505

ULTEX
21 Adley Rd.
Cambridge, Mass. 02138
(800) 343-5080
(617) 491-6744

WILLIAM UNGER
230 Fifth Ave.
New York, N.Y. 10001
(212) 532-0689

WENDY YARNS U.S.A.
P.O. Box 11672
Milwaukee, Wis. 53211

YARN MANUFACTURERS IN THE U.K. AND FRANCE

CHAT BOTTE
BP 34959056
Roubaix
Cedex 1
France

EMU WOOLS
Leeds Road
Greengates
Bradford
West Yorks
U.K.

HAYFIELD MILLS
Glusburn
Nr. Keighley
West Yorks BD20 8QP
U.K.

LISTER-LEE
George Lee & Sons Ltd.
White Oak Mills
P.O. Box 37
Wakefield
West Yorks
U.K.

PHILDAR
4 Gambrel Road
Westgate Industrial Estate
Northampton NN5 5NS
U.K.

SIRDAR LTD.
Flanshaw Lane
Alverthorpe
Wakefield WF2 9ND
U.K.

SUNBEAM
Richard Ingram & Co. Ltd.
Cranshaw Mills
Pudsey LS28 7BS
U.K.

3 SUISSES
Marlborough House
38 Welford Road
Leicester LE2 7AA
U.K.

WENDY INTERN
P.O. Box 3
Guiseley
West Yorks
U.K.